LAW: AN OUTLINE FOR THE
INTENDING STUDENT

CONTRIBUTORS

R. H. Graveson
A. G. Chloros
A. K. R. Kiralfy
C. E. P. Davies
A. G. Guest
A. D. Hughes
A. J. Boyle
T. E. James
Naomi E. Michaels
R. H. Maudsley
G. I. A. D. Draper
M. R. Chesterman
D. B. Parker

LAW

An Outline for the Intending Student

Edited by

Professor R. H. Graveson, Q.C., LL.D.

*Head of the Department and Dean of
the Faculty of Laws of King's College, London*

LONDON

ROUTLEDGE & KEGAN PAUL

First published 1967
by Routledge & Kegan Paul Ltd
Broadway House, 68–74 Carter Lane
London, E.C.4

Printed in Great Britain
by Richard Clay (The Chaucer Press), Ltd
Bungay, Suffolk

CONTENTS

I

Introduction

R. H. Graveson

THE GENERAL INTEREST IN LAW, especially among young people, has grown so much since the end of the war of 1939–45 (and perhaps because of it and its consequences) that my colleagues and I have ventured to offer this elementary introduction to the subject. In so doing, we have had particularly in mind two groups of non-lawyers: pupils at school who are required to participate in general courses of sixth-form study, or who might wish to learn about a possible career; and those about to start the study of law at a university or for the professions, who require some preliminary reading. Beyond these two special groups, we hope that this Outline may be of interest to the general lay public.

Accordingly, it is fair to ask this question: if I were you, what would I wish to know about law? First, I think, I should ask what it is: then, what sort of law are we talking about? what does law do? how does it fit into my own life? and how does it come into existence? If the answers to these questions satisfied me I might then hope to learn something of the organisation of law into branches, of its administration and possibly of its reform. Finally, perhaps, I might wonder about the relation between law and justice, and who are the men and women who make law their career. It is through these imagined questions that this little book has been planned in the hope that it may provide, if not all the answers, at least some guide to further enquiry. My colleagues have dealt with many of these broad questions in the pages which follow.[1] It is for the editor, writing his preface last, to introduce this dialogue between lawyer and layman.

Your first question, what is law? can be answered in a sentence in a minute, or in a hundred volumes over a thousand years, for it is the basic and constant question, as difficult as the nature of truth. The kind of law with which we have to deal in this Outline is that which governs the relations of human beings one with another. It is the body of rules which say how men and women should behave towards each other in society, whether in fact they do behave in such a way or not. It is thus different from scientific laws, which do not say what *should* happen, but what *does* or *will probably* happen in given circumstances. You might compare the laws of gravity or astronomy, which tell us what consequences will follow from certain physical conditions in the world of nature, with the law which says that you should not park your car in a prohibited place, and what may happen if you do so. In a philosophical sense, the law with which we have to deal is not one of the natural sciences but of the so-called normative sciences, laying down what people should do under given circumstances. Yet it may be distinguished from other bodies of normative rules, as of religion, ethics or the rules of a game, in that the particular body of norms with which we shall deal applies to us in an obligatory manner by virtue of our membership of a politically organised society.

The needs of man everywhere and always are conditioned by the stages of birth, life, reproduction, self-preservation and death within a life-cycle of some seventy years and a necessary framework of association with other human beings. This is the context in which provision has to be made for the ordered life of human beings in society. For the purpose of facilitating and organising these processes and stages, human beings are driven from sheer necessity to establish obligatory rules of behaviour. Without such rules they could not co-exist, and it is this essential minimum pattern of obligatory rules of behaviour which lies at the core of what is meant by law. One could go further and deduce that law is not merely an attribute of the living together of human beings in society but in chemical terms an element, in the sense that without law there could be no society at all. When we think of law in the sense of this book we may be led into a modern and sophisticated view of the subject as something that we could read in a statute or the judgment of a court as found in the Law Reports. But law in its original form would certainly not be written and might not even be spoken. It would simply be followed so far as necessary. It probably began as an accepted way of behaviour among human beings which they regarded as essential to the existence and continuance of their living together.

It will thus appear that the purpose for which law is used is basically to make social life possible. Beyond that it may be used for whatever purpose is regarded by society as desirable for achievement. As you will see later, one form of law, probably the most important form today, is statute law, the legislation of Parliament. It is easy to see how the government in power can make effective through passing an Act of Parliament any policy it may hold regarding the social or economic life of the people. In fact, the conversion of policy into law by means of legislation is the normal and obvious process by which a successful political party gives effect to its programme. Perhaps it is worth observing in parentheses that Acts of Parliament, like all law of which we are speaking, are made by men and women like you and me. We are in fact dealing with a human institution with both its faults and its possibilities of improvement, not with something that has come down to us from above and is beyond the reach of human action. The particular rules of law deal with the various situations of human life in society, for example, marriage, divorce, succession, the making of contracts, the sale and acquisition of property, the commission of wrongs such as fraud or murder. A legal system will generalise these situations, and on them base rules of law which indicate the consequences of the action embodied in the situations. The rule of law will usually be formulated on a hypothetical basis, indicating the consequences that can be expected to follow from the occurrence of certain events. Thus the criminal law is for the most part formulated in terms of rules that any person who commits certain acts shall on conviction be guilty of a specified offence; for example, a person who takes and carries away property belonging to another without a claim of right shall be guilty of the offence of larceny. It is interesting to observe that there is no direct prohibition of stealing in the law, but merely a statement of the penal consequences of such action and a definition of the person committing the wrong in terms of the act he has done.

It will be clear from what has been said that there is an intimate relation between fact and law, between the circumstances and the varying facts of human life and the rule of law which is devised to control them. It is considered that law can exist only in relation to fact, real or hypothetical, fictitious or imagined (but still fact), since law has no purpose other than the control of factual situations in social life. This fundamental relationship is reflected at all stages in the history of law. The ancient Greeks evolved the concept of an eternal and universal natural law based on the observation of such natural facts and phenomena as the seasons and the behaviour of the stars. No better example of the relationship of law and fact exists in the contemporary world than in the trial of jury actions at assizes or quarter sessions. The civil claim or the criminal charge will be based on a rule of law embodying a general factual situation. It will be the duty of the plaintiff or the prosecution to bring forward evidence of facts in his particular case which constitute a specific example of the general situation embodied in the rule of law. This is the first element in a trinity of factors which make up a legal decision. The second element is the relevant rule of law which the judge will explain to the jury in summing up the evidence by which the existence of the facts has been proved. Once the facts and the law have been established in their relationship, the third part of the operation can be undertaken, which is a statement of the judgment of the court or the verdict of the jury as a legal conclusion derived from the application of the law to the proven facts. The doors of all English courts are normally open to you without charge, and it is proceedings in them which are the living illustrations of the discussion that follows in this book.

The idea of the social sciences is something fairly new, and differences of opinion exist on whether law should properly be assigned to this area of knowledge. Some of the newer universities regard law as one aspect of the social sciences, to be treated in schools of social science. Most of the older ones tend to reject the view that law properly belongs to the social sciences, an attitude which is based partly on a traditional distrust of social sciences generally and a reluctance to allow an ancient academic discipline to be contaminated by association with such newcomers as sociology, psychology and even economics. But it will have appeared from what has been said that law is not only a social science but possibly the most elemental of them all in its creative function of society itself. To its making goes everything that makes up life, constituents and elements which are best seen in the example of parliamentary legislation embodying political policy to which we have referred. The great American jurist, Roscoe Pound, analysed law in a most helpful and illuminating way when he said that it consisted of legal precepts identifiable in a descending order of abstraction as concepts (for example, negligence), principles (for example, that liability depends on fault rather than causation) and rules (e.g. the penalty for driving a car without due care and attention is a fine of $£x$ or y months' imprisonment), together with two further elements: the received ideals of a particular society, indicating the purpose for which rules of law should be fashioned and used; and what Dean Pound called the taught tradition, a recognition of the historical factor in the training of those who make and administer the law. In the case of English law our rules have gradually evolved and grown up through a centuries-long accretion of judicial decisions. For the most part, the general body of law in the United Kingdom until fifty years ago has been allowed to evolve in a natural and unhurried manner, supplemented by legislation from time to time and particularly when required by the needs of a new government. But the mark of modern times is the greatly extended use of legislation.

The United Kingdom has no Ministry of Justice, such as is found in most Continental countries. One of the tasks of such ministries is to keep watch on foreign legislation for any new ideas for the legal solution of common problems, such as traffic accidents. We have dealt with this aspect of law reform in a somewhat piecemeal fashion in the past by the appointment of law-reform committees or commissions to investigate particular branches of law; but their terms of reference, no less than their success, have been limited. Accordingly, it was something of a notable event in the history of our law when in 1965, by the Law Commissions Act, separate Law Commissions were established for England and Scotland, charged with the reform of their respective legal systems. No longer will it be necessary to await the accident of litigation to raise a particular point before the courts, or for the luck of the draw of Private Members' Bills in Parliament by which changes in the general law may be proposed. English and Scottish law, in any of their respects, can now be subjected to the objective scrutiny of the Law Commissions, the scope of whose work may be judged from the reports published annually, of which the first has already appeared and may be obtained from H.M. Stationery Office. Hope now exists that the law may be able to keep in sight of other social sciences, if not of the natural sciences, in this era of increasing acceleration of human life.

Suggested Reading

Readers should use the latest available edition of any book suggested in this Outline for further reading.

KEETON, G. W., *Elementary Principles of Jurisprudence*, Pitman.

NOTES

1. All contributors to this Outline have been free to express their own views, for which the editor can accept neither credit nor responsibility.

2

Law and Society

A. G. Chloros

LAW SEEMS TO MOST LAYMEN such a specialised field of human activity that their approach to it is often uncertain and hesitant. What the lawyers sometimes call the majesty of the law appears awe-inspiring. On the other hand, the law and the lawyers are frequently shrouded by suspicion and distrust. It is not unusual to come up against the view that the law is something remote from life; that the less one has dealings with it the better. Surely, it may be claimed, law and lawyers are something apart from humanity. After all, are we not familiar with the indignant outburst of Dickens that 'the law is a ass—a idiot' and has not Shakespeare himself proclaimed 'The first thing we do, let's kill all the lawyers'? 'Good jurist, bad Christian,' preached Martin Luther. Indeed, the list of men of literary genius that have attacked the lawyers is long and distinguished. It may come, therefore, as a surprise if it is suggested that there is hardly any other form of human activity that is more human than the law. 'I am a man, I count nothing human indifferent to me,' wrote Terence. This motto could well apply to the lawyer. For, if we try for a moment to move away from popular myths we may ask the question: 'Is there anything, any science or art more concerned with human affairs than the law?' Like M. Jourdain in Molière's *Le Bourgeois Gentilhomme*, who did not know that he was speaking prose, is not man today in his way of life, health and well-being, controlled by law? If we reflect on the role that the law plays in our lives, both private and social, we shall realise that without law, organised society, as we under-

7

stand it, would be impossible, and that our health and happiness depend upon the kind of legal system under which we live. To appreciate this it may be enough to say that from the moment of birth to the moment of death, our lives are regulated by law. Between two legal documents, the birth and the death certificates, our own well-being and our relationship with others are governed by law. A newly born baby is invisibly but effectively protected by law; for it is the law that will establish and safeguard the rights of the parents and of those who can take decisions for his education and upbringing. Later the child will grow and feel his way into society, for no one can have a full life alone as a hermit in the desert. He will wish to marry and raise a family of his own; if his life becomes miserable he may even seek a divorce. He will work and acquire property. In all these cases it is the law that will determine his rights and duties. Though he may never come into contact with a court of law, he will constantly use the services of the law; just as the healthy individual will have to follow the elementary rules of hygiene if he is to remain healthy. If he fails in his obligations towards society it is the law which will protect the other members of society from him. But we must go beyond the limited span of human life if we are to appreciate the full extent of the role of the law; for the law looks after our interests before birth; for example, there is legislation for the protection of the expectant mother; moreover, it is the law that secures the rights of the unborn infant in regard to his personality or his rights of property and succession. At the other end, the law will take into account and regulate our wishes and interests after death, possibly for a long time thereafter.

These observations may give a different view of the law and the lawyers to those who regard law as little scraps of legislation written in incomprehensible jargon and of the lawyers as elderly gentlemen disguised in gowns and wigs and mumbling incantations in sombre courtrooms. In fact, no other branch of social activity is as intensively human as the law, for no other subject invites us, as the law does, to consider all aspects of human life together. It is not surprising that great figures of the past have often applied their minds to the law. 'Justice,' wrote Aristotle, 'is the source of all virtue.' Some of the noblest sentiments of human society have often been expressed in legal documents. Thus, we find the following statement in one of the earliest English legal texts which dates back to the thirteenth century. 'The King himself ought not to be subject to any man, but he ought to be subject to God and the law since law makes the King. Therefore let the King render to the law what the law has rendered to the King, viz. dominion and power for there is no King where will rules and not the law.'[1] It would be difficult to over-emphasise the value of this statement as a principle of action that promotes individual freedom. If we go back in history even farther we find that the Romans had already pronounced upon law and justice. Perhaps in the most famous introductory book for law students ever written,[2] Justinian defines justice as 'the set and constant purpose which gives to everyman his due'. The law is the practical expression of justice, for 'the precepts of the law are these: to live honestly, to injure no one and to give every man his due.' It is not surprising that such a highly moral view of the law leads Justinian to declare, with understandable exaggeration, that 'Jurisprudence is the knowledge of things divine and human, the science of the just and the unjust.'[3]

Whatever the definition, law is in effect a vital function of society, one may say even an indispensable one. It can indeed be claimed that those thinkers who at some time or other imagined the perfect society as a lawless society were wrong and their thinking utopian. We may regard, perhaps, the ideal of a lawless society as evidence of dissatisfaction with social conditions and existing law, but we cannot take it more seriously than that. If Voltaire was able to dispense with law in his magic land Eldorado, which he describes so eloquently in his book *Candide*, it is the most dangerous, but also the most fruitless, practice to attempt to dispense with law. Marxism, for example, is still in theory based upon the maxim that in the communist society law and the State will wither away. When at the time of the Russian

Revolution some tried to put this maxim into effect the attempt failed miserably. Though lawyers as a professional class were liquidated, law survived. Indeed, after the Revolution, law became far stricter than it was, for a revolutionary society in a state of flux requires stricter measures and tighter control than a peaceful and socially coherent state. It is not, therefore, surprising that every revolution which began by eliminating lawyers, in Arnold Bennett's terms 'as the most vicious opponents of social progress', ended up with the re-establishment of the legal profession.

Law and the Sciences

To appreciate the function of law in society fully it is not enough merely to establish that a close contact exists between them. The place of law in society is a far more complex and subtle problem which requires not only detailed knowledge of the law but also a study of the periphery or the background of the law. For the principles of behaviour that we consider vital to our lives in society are affected by the law in two ways: they determine the kind of law that we have, but are themselves also profoundly influenced by the law. This is another way of saying that law reflects society but also, up to a point, controls it. A great deal of investigation has been carried out in this field in the last hundred years, particularly in the United States, which is the home of the so-called 'Sociological School', but, of course, the process of investigation is as old as Plato and Aristotle. In fact, Plato in his *Republic* and Aristotle in his *Politics* were concerned with the kind of law that would be most suitable in the perfect society. In modern times biology and psychology have shown that the law must be sensitive to new discoveries. To give an example or two, progress in psychology may directly affect legal ideas relating to the law of insanity. At what point, one may ask, is a person insane and therefore not responsible for his acts? Ever since the killing of Sir Robert Peel's Secretary by a lunatic called M'Naghten, the law has been based upon a moral rather than a medical test—did he know what he was doing, and if so, did he know he was doing wrong? The law now recognises degrees of insanity, or as the law puts it 'diminished responsibility'. In the treatment of criminals account has also been taken of background and environment. The objects of punishment have altered, and though expiation is still part of our law, there has been a distinct change towards reform. There are Borstal institutions and after-care of released prisoners. But if much work has been done in the field of Criminal law a lot of investigation and research is necessary in other branches of the law. For example, what kind of behaviour must the law take into account as being decisive in the breakdown of matrimonial relations leading to a divorce? It is also clear that progress in medicine has enabled the lawyer to apply certain presumptions to claims of paternity in the case of a child conceived outside wedlock.

New scientific inventions pose new problems, such as the sovereignty and control of outer space. With a view to the future, the lawyer must also take into account the development of mechanical civilisation. He must ascertain whether computers and electronic brains can be put to routine use in those aspects of the law which belong much more to administration than to litigation. In all these points of contact between law and the sciences it is obvious that the lawyer will have a vital role to play.

Law and Morality

In discussing these questions the lawyer will find himself face to face with the problem of values. For law not only depends upon but also contains a scale of values: those of the society in which it operates. But if we speak of values are we not already involved in a discussion which has a strong theological context? Religious beliefs and theological doctrines have certainly been influential in this field, for the Church has always stood for what it describes as the sovereignty of the moral law, a law that can be used as a criterion of human conduct and human law. Others, outside religion, believe in the moral or natural law, not as emanating from a superior and divine Being but from the rational nature of man. As Hugo Grotius, the seventeenth-century jurist wrote: 'Even God cannot cause that two times two should not make four.'[5] Obviously, these problems cannot be discussed in depth without a knowledge of the law. But their examination suggests that law, far from being a closed science, is very much in the centre of society.

It may be asked more precisely, in what way does a scale of values affect law? Two answers come readily to mind. First, the current ideas about right and wrong must necessarily determine the principles of the law. Secondly, a scale of values is decisive in shaping the kind of state in which we live and ultimately the liberty and happiness of all citizens. It is in this spirit that the American Constitution guarantees life, liberty and the pursuit of happiness. But one is tempted to ask here, who's happiness, or which morality? Is it the duty of the law to enforce its own morality, which is also the morality of the State? Or must private morality also be taken into account, and if so to what extent? It may well be asked how far is the State justified in imposing its own moral standards upon its citizens? A great deal has been written about this problem recently, and it is not surprising that the lawyers have been much exercised by it.[6] Is there a private morality in which the State must not interfere? Must the State legislate to stop us from taking drugs, or getting drunk or maintaining a mistress, even though we may keep our activities to ourselves and do no harm to others? Or has the State a right to be the custodian of morality, as the House of Lords thought recently in a case in which some persons had published a 'Ladies Directory'?[7]

There may be, as some writers think, a public and a private morality with intersecting circles, and it may be right for the State to interfere within the area of public morality. But then the further question arises, by what standards is the distinction to be drawn as between *public* and *private* morality? On the other hand, to admit that individuals should be entirely free to act as they wish so long as they do no harm to others, may lead to a type of society which is entirely different from the society in which we are accustomed to live. For example, on the basis of this argument of complete freedom, it is arguable that polygamy, divorce, drug-taking, abortion and euthanasia should be freely resorted to as long as those affected are freely consenting adults.

Moral standards are equally applicable to the international field. Indeed, the generally recognised principles of human behaviour have been recognised in the International Convention of Human Rights and Fundamental Freedoms of 1956. That Convention is not merely a formal declaration of principles, for it has set up an International Court in which an aggrieved individual may seek redress.

Law and Philosophy

Quite obviously the function of the lawyer must include more than a discussion of the legal aspects of morality, however important these may be. His function is greater, in that he must make a synthesis, as best he can and however inadequately, of all the branches of knowledge that have a bearing upon law. He must see the personal problem not as a case, as one may be tempted to do, but as part of a whole and in its true proportions. It is not surprising that the lawyer may be tempted to create his own theories and turn himself into a philosopher, just as the great philosophers have frequently written as lawyers and jurists. Nor is it strange that on occasions the special idiosyncrasies, beliefs and background of these lawyers have helped to give to their theories a peculiar and original flavour. In fact, lawyers have had to group all these different ways of thinking into a special subject of careful study, one which is variously described as Jurisprudence, legal theory or legal philosophy. It would be a mistake to imagine that this is a topic in which lawyers play at being philosophers. For the lawyers have spent their lives in the practice of the law. Thus they have acquired a unique knowledge and experience of human problems which help them to give to their theories a special, practical outlook. Knowledge of the law is a starting-point that a philosopher cannot often hope to achieve. Inevitably, the theories sometimes clash with one another. Many of them, however, make a special contribution to the knowledge of the law, for they show the law in a light not previously seen by others. If a theory does not represent the whole truth, at least it shows one or more facets of the truth. Thus, in the last resort the study of the law is an intellectual exercise of the highest order.

Law and Politics

If lawyers and jurists are inclined to produce theories of their own this does not mean that they are not themselves influenced by general trends and prevailing currents in philosophical or political thinking. In fact, political doctrines which have a bearing upon the conduct of man as a social unit have frequently affected legal practice. An obvious example is the effect of the Marxist doctrine that the ownership of the means of production belongs to the State. Whether an individual shall be allowed to own a factory or not is ultimately a political, not a legal, question. Equally, the question to what extent a person should be entitled to the fruits of his labour cannot be decided until the fundamental principle or, as we might say, the political or social structure of a particular society, can be determined. But when the decisions of principle have been taken it is the lawyers that will have to translate them into practice, and it is through his contacts with the law that the individual will become aware of these decisions. Though he may know little of legal theory, he is certainly likely to ask legal questions if his property is taken away, or its use restricted, or compensation denied. It may be asserted that ultimately the very nature of our lives is decided by what are social and political, but at the same time legal, questions.

In medieval times it was fashionable to speak of the theories of sovereignty, of the divine rights of the King, or of the claims of the Church over secular authority. More recently, theorists have spoken of the doctrine of separation of powers, constitutional government and human rights. All these ideas were expressed in legal documents. It was one of the greatest English Judges, Chief Justice Sir Edward Coke, who, in the seventeenth century, haughtily replied to the King that 'The King in his own person cannot adjudge any case, either criminal or betwixt party and party; but it ought to be determined and adjudged by some Court of Justice according to the law and custom of England'.[8] It is the law, in fact, that provides the machinery for the application of all these ideas. But this does not necessarily mean that law in itself is always good. Whether law is good or bad depends upon our subjective judgment of the principles of a legal system, and of their practical application. For example, in Nazi Germany we may claim law was bad, for it deprived those to whom it applied of what we generally considered as the minimum but indispensable guarantees of a decent life. Thus, we may say that law is not an end in itself but merely, as a famous German lawyer, Rudolf von Jhering, put it in the nineteenth century, a means to an end. Early in our century Pound, the leader of the American Sociological School, expressed the same idea when he said that law is a means of social control.

Though some lawyers have tried to isolate law from its social context and create an abstract structure of logical rules entirely independent from the society to which they applied, this attempt has been a failure. It was a distinguished American judge, Oliver Wendell Holmes, who best expressed the futility of isolating law when he said that 'the life of the law is not logic but experience';[9] or as Jhering explained in a humorous but very profound work, in the after-life there is a paradise of pure legal concepts that work perfectly, like machines, in absolute darkness. They are perfect because they have no connection whatsoever with life; and they work in darkness because daylight, the light of society, is not allowed to contaminate them.[10]

Law as a Social Science

If law is in effect a social science we must look for the points of contact between law and the other social sciences, for one affects the other. The difficulty is that the lawyer

15

cannot hope to achieve mastery in all the other social sciences as well as in the law. Life is too short for what has been described as 'megalomaniac' jurisprudence.[11] What is certainly feasible, nevertheless, is that the lawyer should become aware of the importance of the social sciences and, wherever possible, seek the advice of or work closely with other social scientists. Here it is best to take a concrete example. Since the beginning of our century some of the most significant advances have occurred in psychology. Freud discovered psycho-analysis, and its impact was felt strongly upon all other sciences. These advances tended to suggest that human behaviour is determined by factors that are independent from our will. The individual, it was claimed, is guided by his subconscious, by a complex of desires and fears. Environment is decisive in the upbringing of children. Some went so far as to claim that the notion of free will, so much exalted by the German philosopher Kant, was outmoded or misconceived. New doctrines arose—behaviourism and existentialism—suggesting directly or indirectly and in different ways that responsibility for evil or anti-social acts may not lie in the individual. But our legal systems were based upon the notion of fault. As the French Civil Code lays down in a famous article, 'Any act whatever of a person which causes damage to another obliges the person through whose fault it has occurred to reparation.'[12] The rule that 'you are to love your neighbour,' said an English Judge, in a case which has now become a classic, 'becomes in law, you must not injure your neighbour and the question who is my neighbour receives a restricted reply. You must take reasonable care to avoid acts or omissions which you can reasonably foresee would be likely to injure your neighbour.'[13] All other legal systems have similar provisions.

If it is true that the behaviour of an individual is guided by factors beyond his control, are we not too hard in applying an objective standard of judgment to carelessness, that of the abstract reasonable man, or as a judge once said, of 'the man on the Clapham Omnibus'? We need only apply this line of argument to one field of human misery imposed upon us by the development of mechanical civilisation, that of motor accidents, to realise the extent to which our view of responsibility is decisive in establishing liability in law. If there is no such thing as fault, why should motorists be held responsible for carelessness? The development of insurance in many fields of life has tended to make this problem even more complex, for in the particular instance a careless, but insured, motorist need not pay any compensation. His fault is irrelevant to his purse. It is significant that voices have recently been raised in France suggesting that motor accidents should be taken completely out of the law of responsibility and placed in the law of insurance.[14] Whatever the moral arguments against this view, it is undeniable that this solution would be most convenient, for it would wipe out thousands of disputes which in most cases are in fact disputes between insurance companies.

Law from Within

If the impression is given here that through the study of law in society the individual obtains what the Germans aptly call a *Weltanschauung*, a view of the world, it should equally be observed that it is also possible to look at law from within. It is in this respect that contemporary studies in general philosophy have been extended to the analysis of the law. We have become aware of the significance of words; it is through the use of words that we can communicate thought as well as legislate rules of conduct. But if we misuse the words communication becomes difficult, if not impossible. As Humpty Dumpty said in *Alice in Wonderland*, 'When I use a word it means just what I choose it to mean . . .' Thus, some philosophers have tried to determine the exact meaning of words and legal terms. In fact, the idea that the meaning of words changes according to the context in which they are used is not a new one. The Greek philosopher Heraclitus had already observed that you cannot point to the same river twice. The meaning of words, like a river, is in a constant state of flux. What, then, is the modern philosopher's function? A modern philosopher in the field of linguistic analysis, Wittgenstein, suggests that it is to define words in the context in which they are used; or, as he puts it, to show the fly the way out of the bottle. But others, starting from different premises, have also shown extreme suspicion of words, and in particular of the printed words in the books. The so-called American realists have claimed that the belief in the certainty and the validity of abstract rules of law is a 'father complex' shared by the lawyers and that only a complete scientific investigation into the nature of the judicial system can provide an adequate explanation of the law. It is far better, they claim, to analyse the judicial process, that is to study the specific circumstances of a trial, the psychology of the Judge, of the lawyers and of the jurors, than to look at the abstract formulation of the law which is supposed, often erroneously, to apply to a case. There is no better way of illustrating this school of thought than to quote the words of an American judge, who became a famous exponent of the realist theory: 'So the judge's sympathies and antipathies are likely to be active with respect to the persons of the witness, the attorneys and the parties to the suit. His own past may have created plus or minus reactions to women, or blonde women, or men with beards, or Southerners, or Italians, or Englishmen, or plumbers, or ministers, or college graduates, or Democrats.'[15] And he concludes 'If the personality of the judge is the principal factor in law administration, then law may vary with the personality of the judge who happens to pass upon any given case.'[16] There is certainly some substance in these claims, for the mere fact that a dispute has come before a court means that there is room for doubt and interpretation. Moreover, just like an illness, a law-suit may represent a breakdown in the smooth regulation of society. But it would be wrong to conclude that the judges enjoy complete freedom to decide each case according to their ideas of right and wrong; for in that case not only would the judge have become, as Hobbes said, a sovereign legislator but any regulation of life through legislation would be impossible. For the function of the law is far greater than that of deciding individual cases: it is to be a guide for the future. To judge the law merely from the cases is like judging the healthy body from patients in hospitals. Law in the last resort must remain a body of rules regulating future conduct. Another attack against the rule theory of the law has come from the Scandinavian realists. They have also shown suspicion towards legal forms as having a magical rather than a rational significance. The essence of law, they claim, is that certain precepts when translated into law acquire a magical significance, for they provide the key to our psychological mechanism of obedience, just like the incantations of the witch doctors. They are effective because they have come from the witch doctor. The Scandinavian School seems to have used recent discoveries in psychology to good effect. But one wonders whether ultimately to ascribe obedience of the law to psychological reasons is to solve rather than to state the problem.

The Nature of Law

It may be a paradox that the discussion of the place of law in society ends up with the realisation that law is a far more complex phenomenon than it was thought at first. It is not surprising that it was a philosopher, Plato, who first asked the questions 'what is law?' and 'what is justice?' A layman's view of law in terms of police action or as an activity which is obscure and remote from life must, by the nature of things, be somewhat misconceived. However, it can be asserted that no other single science or art can be as close to life as law. Napoleon had well understood this when he wrote from St. Helena, that: 'My true glory is not to have won 40 battles. . . . My defeat at Waterloo will erase the memory of so many victories but what nothing will destroy, what will live for ever, is my Civil Code.'[19] The subsequent expansion of the French code to many parts of the world fully justified his prophecy. Equally, the Common law of England was expounded in large parts of the world and is still a living influence not only in the United States but in many other lands that have completely severed their links with England; just as the survival of Roman culture in the modern world owes a great deal to the influence that Roman law, and in particular Justinian's codification, has had upon Europe.

Indeed, one may go further, without exaggeration, and declare that there is no safer way of understanding the character, history and customs of a people than through the study of its legal system. For the hopes, fears and psychology as well as the social structure of a country are admirably reflected in its laws.

The increase of the speed and the facility of communication from country to country and from continent to continent which are typical features of our time are imposing upon the modern lawyer a further duty, that of the study of other proximate legal systems. Problems with an international flavour are becoming more numerous than before. For example, a person is born in England of foreign parents; he may marry a foreign citizen and obtain a divorce in yet another country. He may make a will outside England and leave property in several countries. It is not surprising that those branches of the law which are particularly concerned with such problems, Conflict of laws and Comparative law, have increasingly come into prominence. If the study of other systems was a luxury in the past, it has become a vital need of our time, for the advances in science and technology have made our world much smaller than it was. There is greater need for understanding and greater need for legal uniformity. To cross a frontier is to cross into a different world, a world which has its own charm because it is different, but also a world which becomes difficult to live in if there is diversity of legal regulation. Hence there is constant need for legal interpretation and unification in the world of today, and the groupings that several nations have formed, such as the Common Market, have made it increasingly necessary to look at their social problems and their legal rules, not in the narrow nationalistic terms of the past, but within a broader framework. This process will undoubtedly continue, and the lawyer's task will correspondingly become more difficult, but perhaps also more satisfying. That task is to view law not as an isolated and abstract phenomenon but as an instrument of policy and social control; also to adapt the law to new social conditions beyond the frontier of his country without at the same time destroying the essential character and unity of the law. For the eternal dilemma of the law has always been how to provide the stability that society requires while adjusting itself to the continuous process of social change.

Suggested Reading

C. K. ALLEN, *Law in the Making*, Oxford University Press.
B. CARDOZO, *The Nature of the Judicial Process*, Yale Paperboard.
D'ENTRÈVES, *Natural Law*, Hutchinson's Library.
LORD DEVLIN, *The Enforcement of Morals*, Oxford University Press.
W. FRIEDMANN, *Law in a Changing Society*, Pelican.
C. J. FRIEDRICH, *The Philosophy of Law in Historical Perspective*, University of Chicago Press.
DENNIS LLOYD, *The Idea of Law*, Pelican.

NOTES

[1] Bracton, *Tractatus de legibus* f.5.b.
[2] *Institutes* I.I. (Moyle's translation).
[3] *Ibid.*
[4] Homicide Act, 1957 S.2 (37 *Halsbury's Statutes* (2nd ed.) 174).
[5] *De Jure Belli et Pacis I*, i. x. para 1 (Kelsey's translation in the series of Classics of International Law). But Grotius merely posed the question. He was not himself a rationalist.
[6] See, e.g., Lord Devlin, *The Enforcement of Morals* (1965).
[7] *Shaw v. Director of Public Prosecutions* (1961) 2. W.L.R. 897.
[8] *Prohibitions del Roy*, 12 Co. Rep. 63 (1607).
[9] *The Common Law* (1881) 1.
[10] Scherz und Ernst in der Jurisprudenz (Im Begriffshimmel—ein Fantasiebild).
[11] C. K. Allen, *Law in the Making* (1946) 35 Oxford University Press.
[12] Art. 1382.
[13] Lord Atkin in *Donoghue v. Stevenson* (1932) A.C. 562, 580.
[14] See André Tunc, 'The Twentieth Century Development and Function of the Law of Torts in France', *International and Comparative Law Quarterly* (1965) xiv, 1089.
[15] Jerome Frank, *Law and the Modern Mind* (1949) 106.
[16] *Ibid.* 111.
[17] Schwarz (ed.), *The Code Napoleon and the Common Law world* (1956) 102.

3

The Structure of a
Legal System

A. K. R. Kiralfy

General

IN MODERN SOCIETIES law is laid down by legislative bodies,
like the Parliament of the United Kingdom, or under their
authority, as in the case of regulations made by Departments
of Government, or by courts of justice in the course of deciding actual cases, like the High Court of Justice in London
stating the principles of law on which a decision is based.
The rules of law so laid down are embodied, in the case of
legislatures, in statutes or codes of law or bodies of regulations and, in the case of courts, in the relevant portions of
the judgment given by the court and published in a series
of law reports. Hence every court which refers to the law
must have a library of statutes and law reports.

In many foreign countries which follow the Roman law
tradition much weight is attached to the opinions of academic writers who put forward proposed solutions to legal
problems or comment on the meaning of codes and statutes.
In England, the United States and most of the Commonwealth the judge's opinion is relied on rather than that of
the professor of law, though the judge may be influenced
by academic writings on the subject with which he is dealing.

In many small communities the same *élite* acts as a legislative, executive and judicial body. It makes laws, enforces
them and sits in judgment on those who violate them. In
more advanced societies this becomes impossible and there

is a more efficient division of function. Thus the group of counsellors around the English Kings gradually separated during the Middle Ages into advisers on policy, professional full-time judges, ambassadors and civil servants. In many foreign countries there is a dogmatic 'separation of powers', and the main functions of the State are rigidly divided among different groups; for example, in the United States the American Congress acts as a legislature, the President and his own nominees as an executive, and the Supreme Court as a judiciary.[1] In England this is less rigidly observed, but the functions of Parliament are basically to introduce fundamentally new laws and set up new institutions, whereas the judges are left to work out the rules governing existing social relations, so far as they are unaffected by statutes passed by Parliament, and to apply and interpret the statutes. Their training and experience make them particularly well suited to this task.

Judge-made Law

'Judge-made law' or 'case law' is especially typical of the English legal system and those systems based upon it. The main principles of English law had to be settled during the later Middle Ages when parliaments met infrequently and even then showed little interest in private law problems. A judge may never refuse to decide a case because of a supposed absence of legal authority on which to do so—indeed, this principle is expressly stated in some foreign codes of law. The judge must, if necessary, himself devise a rule to fit the facts, in order to complete his decision. Constitutional niceties are preserved by the theory that the judge acts as a kind of legislative agent. The legislature can certainly overrule his decision by enacting a different rule for the future and even for the past, but this is only usual where big social interests are affected, for example the status of trade unions or the eviction of large numbers of tenants of flats. In the main the judge is allowed to continue to make law much as in earlier times, except that the field of non-statutory law is shrinking much faster, so that he spends most of his time expounding statutes rather than inventing new principles

Much of our law of civil liability is still judge-made. In its formulation the judges drew on contemporary conditions and practices and responded to stimuli from the public. Thus, they did not lay down any broad ideas of a law of contract in advance, but dealt with numerous disputes on the details of contracts already entered into, producing general principles by generalising from the results. The terms of the contract and the status of the parties supplied them with firm data to begin with, for example, descriptions of goods, dates of delivery, age of parties. In the same way the law of tort was not established as an ideal code but evolved slowly and painfully from decisions on many disputes arising out of actual misfortunes, for example, trespasses to land, libels and the like. The court had data such as the fact of publication of a libel and its results or the boundaries of land and the entry on the land by the defendant, and, in modern running-down cases, data like speed, direction and breach of traffic regulations. Typical of judge-made law is the idea of liability being for fault, for failure by the defendant to observe a moral standard, since such a test protected the court from criticism by citizens, who might otherwise have objected to the practice of allowing judges to make rules binding upon them.

In the fields of criminal law, local government law, taxation, land transfer and many others statute is dominant, but the courts approach the interpretation of these enactments on the basis of the legal background and tradition which the draftsmen of the texts of the statutes also share—training at the English Bar. They also examine them impartially, without commitment to the intention of the Government or concern with speeches in the Houses of Parliament.

The words of statutes, like the words of other documents, are often clear enough on the face of them, and yet their effect when an actual situation arises is not at all clear and requires judicial analysis in the light of the context of the statute and the objects of its enactment. Is a bicycle a 'vehicle'? Is a paved road at a dockside a 'highway'? Is a driver 'using' his car on the road when he is pushing it along to try to start it, or when he leaves it on the road without an engine? It has sometimes been said that no one knows what a statute means until it has been interpreted by the courts, and Ministers of the Crown who are proposing some new section of a statute will sometimes tell an unruly Member to consult his lawyer if he asks them what it means.

Judicial Precedent

It is characteristic of the informal character of our law at the summit that no statute was ever passed giving the decisions of courts the authority of law or requiring other courts to follow them. The judges have never admitted that they create law, holding that they merely state what was already in existence, much as the sculptor has sometimes been said to 'bring out' the statue already waiting in the stone. The 'common law' of England is conceived of as a pre-existing body of general custom equipped to solve all legal problems. Statements of law by courts are supposed to be expositions of this custom by men specially equipped by their training for the purpose. But if this law exists it must be uniform: one judge cannot declare it to be one thing and another judge another. Hence our judges' power to make law is limited to situations where no rule has previously been declared. The idea of following precedent is thus not the basis of judge-made law but a brake on its creation. At first precedent was almost irrelevant, since the courts had well-defined jurisdictions and sat in benches consisting of all members of the court. Such courts would naturally decide cases consistently with their own previous decisions. Where jurisdictions overlapped and conflicts of decisions arose an appeal to a higher tribunal would result in uniformity being re-established. From this a further principle of precedent derived, that of the hierarchy of courts, the authority of the higher court to 'correct' the misstatement of law of which the lower court had been guilty. Appeals to higher courts are much commoner in modern times than formerly, so much so that few decisions of courts of first instance are now reported, especially as these courts are now held by a single judge and the likelihood of conflicts among the decisions of numerous trial judges is much greater. Of course they avoid them where possible and try to follow each other's rulings if they happen to know of them.

It will be obvious that judge-made law suffers from a serious built-in disadvantage, that it is a 'one-way street'. Parliament may constantly revise its laws, but once the highest court has given its ruling on some point the law is settled for all time, unless Parliament can be induced to change it. English appellate courts have in the last decades declared themselves bound by their own previous decisions, for the sake of certainty and to maintain the fiction that they were merely declaring some rule already existing but unrevealed outside themselves. In the summer of 1966, however, the Lord Chancellor, Lord Gardiner, stated that the House of Lords, our highest court, intended to be free to alter its own previous rulings in those exceptional cases where it felt that a mistake had been made. It is imagined that this power will be used only where a decision has been widely disapproved by foreign courts or our own academic or professional opinion. Even this relaxation of principle does not alter the illogical operation of all judge-made law, that it imposes liability or inflicts punishment after the fact for something which was not obviously wrong before it. Jeremy Bentham described judge-made law as like the law you make for your dog—you let him misbehave and then punish him as a warning for the future.

Law Reporting

An English law library contains a large collection of volumes of law reports, published chronologically, some of them dating back to the time of King Henry VIII. There has never been a regular official series, probably because only a selection of cases is worth reporting, and it would be too expensive to report more. Only a few cases embody statements of legal principle likely to be useful in the future; the great majority turning on disputes of fact.

The disorderly nature of chronological reports made it necessary to supplement them with digests and encyclopaedias arranged by subject-matter, and by text-books which collect and co-ordinate the decisions in order to provide for lawyers a means of ready reference to the authorities.

Character of Case Law

Case law is extremely rich and sophisticated, being based on a large number of individual instances. It is also practical and close to life, since the cases litigated affect real people in current transactions under contemporary conditions. On the other hand, it is necessarily casual and fragmentary and appears to have little philosophical basis. In particular, the results of a case-law development in one field are often inconsistent with those in another: for example, the line between infancy and majority has been drawn differently in civil and criminal law; undue influence which would invalidate a contract may not affect a will; the sale of a dangerously ruinous house does not attract the liability attaching to the sale of a dangerously damaged revolver. Much of the impetus to law reform has come from these glaring inconsistencies within the general body of the law itself rather than from outside criticism of legal rules.

Case Law Abroad

Judge-made law has not developed to any comparable extent outside the Anglo-American legal world. The strong prejudice felt against it in Europe is linked historically with semi-mythical risings in the Greece and Rome of antiquity against the monopoly of issuing legal edicts enjoyed by a priestly or aristocratic *élite*. The Roman Emperors, on the other hand, prohibited reliance on judicial decisions because their judges were less expert in the law than the jurists who prepared legal opinions and because local judges might not adhere closely enough to the Imperial laws. In modern Europe and in countries with European traditions, there is little room left for purely judge-made law, and even the decisions of courts as to the meaning of statutes do not bind other courts. Needless to say, in practice, practitioners will normally follow the rulings of the highest courts (for example, the French Court of Cassation), while volumes of law reports are issued and decisions of courts are constantly referred to in the pages of legal text-books. At times these decisions are even followed in preference to the solemn wording of statutes which appear to state the contrary.

A middle course between the two extremes is followed in Soviet Russia. It is not the practice there to be bound by any individual decision (though the decisions of the highest courts are regularly reported); the full complement of members of the Supreme Court periodically analyse and collate a series of decisions in some field and then issue a directive commenting on the decisions and instructing the courts in future to follow one line of cases rather than another or to apply one of several possible interpretations of the meaning of some language in a code or statute. Sometimes the case law in an entire field, like the law of succession or of landlord and tenant, is dealt with, so as to provide an authoritative commentary on the statute involved.

Statute Law

Analytically statute law is the classic form of legislation, though historically it has often been the latest to appear. There have been many rivals to its primacy. Mosaic and Islamic law invoke divine inspiration for their texts. Custom had a strong hold in medieval times. Such imagined systems as the Law of Nature or the Law of God have claimed superiority to the ordinary law. The idea of the Law of Nature may have been responsible for the conception of the 'unconstitutional law' which exists in the United States, where the Supreme Court has asserted the right to disallow laws passed by the Federal Congress or the State legislatures as inconsistent with entrenched principles of the Constitution. In England the law-giver is sovereign and uncontrolled; indeed, our modern Parliament has far wider powers than the kings in former times, though it combines within it a number of elements, as will be seen in the next chapter.

At one time statutes were the result of private petitions, but in modern times legislative Bills are normally drafted inside the Government to meet the requirements of Ministries and Departments. Private Members of Parliament are sometimes able to initiate legislation, but this is often turned over to the official draftsmen for better formulation. Legislation is often preceded by consultation with representatives of interested groups, or foreshadowed in the recommendations of Royal Commissions and other bodies set up to consider the present state of some part of the law and recommend its reform, and in Government White Papers, which state Government policy in the light of those recommendations. Law reform is systematically undertaken by various special bodies set up by the Government, such as the present Law Commission, and changes in the law then take statutory form, often in enactments styled 'Law Reform Acts'.

The rate of acceleration of change in a modern community is so high that most development of the law is now achieved through statutes. Statutes which have served their purpose can be amended or repealed at any time and replaced by others, without waiting, as in the case of case law, for the accidents of litigation. It is also fairer that rules of law, which affect the whole public, should be laid down at the cost of Government funds and out of general taxes, rather than at the cost of some individual party or company which happens to become involved in a dispute to which that rule of law applies. The preparation of new legislation can also be conducted at leisure and with full consideration of the consequences, whereas rules of case law are laid down hurriedly and in the heat of the working day in court, in cases sandwiched among many others which, though raising no fine points of law, are equally important and equally time-consuming.

On the other hand, statutes are inflexible and cannot be adapted gradually to meet new conditions. Our modern statutes are also worded in conventionalised technical language which is often obscure, and the judge is not permitted to examine the purpose of the legislature in most cases or to consider the preliminary discussions and recommendations on which the ultimate statute was based. In many statutes it is impossible to extract any general principle which will aid in its detailed interpretation. It is even more difficult to justify provisions of different statutes, drafted on different instructions, which reflect inconsistent ideas, often in closely related fields. Many statutes reflect the ideas current at the time they were passed, but tend to remain overlong in force because they cause insufficient general dissatisfaction to justify the time and trouble needed for their replacement.

Codification

Codification is the restatement of the whole of the law on some subject or on all subjects in substitution for all prior legal rules, statutory and judge-made. It was largely forced on many European countries, such as France and Germany, in order to unify their legal systems, which had previously consisted of large numbers of different bodies of customary law prevailing in different provinces or cities. In the course of this unification choices were made among conflicting rules and the opportunity was taken to provide a general consistent basis for the law, such as individual freedom of will or sanctity of property. A codification is more than a mere quantity of statutory rules, since it involves reducing the law to order, arranging it systematically, prescribing carefully considered solutions for legal problems and finding the right words in which to express them. Its language must be narrow enough to indicate basic principles, yet broad enough to allow flexibility, since no legislature can foresee and solve the problems with which the future is fraught. Many codes confine themselves to generalities and leave details to be laid down by inferior legislation which can be more easily altered from time to time without violating the spirit of the code itself. Tampering with parts of a code may produce just the inconsistency the code was meant to eliminate. Naturally all codes need revision, and the provision made for this is often inadequate. Hence separate statutes have to be passed to modify the law of the code until such time as the code itself can be redrafted or replaced, if ever.

The unity of English law achieved soon after the Norman Conquest has obviated the need for unification by codification, but there are some who would now favour codification, though they are still a minority. Our present system is so complex that it requires a highly skilled but expensive legal profession and eminent but rare judicial capacity. A codified system would impose less need for elaborate research into the law. The opportunity could also be taken to decide what main ideas our law should now embody and to harmonise all our rules with these. Considerable bodies of English law have indeed been successfully codified for use in India and parts of Africa, for example, criminal law, procedure, evidence and commercial law, where certainty is more desirable than complication. The United States, where fifty sovereign States have their own courts, suffers from such indigestibility of sources of law that an unofficial restatement of the fundamentals of American law has been undertaken and enjoys some authority. Many experts, however, feel that codification would be a waste of effort in England and that a flexible body of case law administered by highly experienced judges is more practical and adaptable under English conditions.

Custom

So far nothing has been said of custom as a principal source of law. Of course in modern times events move too swiftly to allow custom much scope, but it has had an important historical role to play and is still vital in many of the less-developed countries. It has also a certain political and philosophical interest. The pre-Conquest law in England was local Saxon custom, and custom was the basis of the law of much of Northern Europe in past centuries. Custom was marked by general voluntary observance; its rules were obeyed because they were law rather than because some official body had prescribed them. Some of it was based on statutes now lost, some of it on orders given by superiors, some of it on plain convenience, but all of it enjoyed actual obedience within its narrow confines. As people were illiterate, customs were for a long time only orally preserved and, if disputed, had to be proved by the testimony of witnesses in a court. The Norman Conquest discouraged the survival of custom in England, but it remained important in France and Germany until modern times and still applies in parts of Spain. In England the law applied in the royal courts was called 'the common custom of the realm' and was deliberately made to grow at the expense of local custom.

To modern people familiar with the almost daily passing of new laws, it may seem strange that in former times law was regarded as divine and unchanging. We have all heard the rather exaggerated reference to the unalterable laws of the Medes and Persians. We know that in medieval times the power of a political ruler to alter long-established custom was doubted, especially if it reflected a delicate balance of forces which might not rashly be disturbed. But custom did change from generation to generation, the lack of written formulations making it easier to lose sight of the fact. Modern European scholars who have visited backward tribes at intervals of time have returned with quite different statements of their customs, although the natives themselves stoutly denied that their customs were or indeed could be changed. In medieval England the grateful King often conferred the 'customs of London' on a generous borough, and the French introduced 'the customs of Paris', again as being the most advanced and advantageous, into New France, to form the basis of much of the civil law of Quebec Province in Canada today.

The English judges presumed that the common law, which they were elaborating, applied everywhere until the contrary was proved. They prohibited the birth of new customs after the year 1189, the date of the accession of Richard the Lion-hearted, which they defined as the 'beginning of legal memory'. They also required all alleged customs to pass a test of 'reasonableness' imposed by themselves, and they could reject a custom they disliked on the pretext that the witnesses had failed to satisfy them of its existence.

Direct survivals of customary law in England are rare: for example, a right of local fishermen to dry nets on a beach or of parishioners to cross a field in order to reach the parish church. But custom has considerable indirect force. It is well known in commercial matters, where mercantile custom has open legal force, but even in other matters it inevitably infiltrates into the body of the law because of the permissive character of English law, that is the assumption that everything that is not forbidden is permitted. Thus two men may enter into some transaction and draw up appropriate documents; if a dispute arises the court will have to deal with it and thus begin to develop rules which would not have been thought of had these two private citizens not come to this arrangement. Custom also enters into our common legal tests of what a reasonable man would do or what a person might reasonably foresee. To drive on the wrong side of the road would certainly be careless if everyone drives on the other side. And a solicitor or physician is judged liable for negligence if he fails to act as solicitors or physicians usually act, rather than for failing to conform to some abstract, ideal standard.

Whereas our customs are based on geographical situation, some legal systems recognise personal customs: for example, marriages may be judged by the religion of the parties and not necessarily by the law of the land where they live.

Some systems of law have been more liberal in recognising the force of custom than we have: for example, Roman law permitted a contrary custom to develop even if it contradicted laws passed by an autocratic emperor, and Islamic law allows a custom to be recognised which is in conflict with the Koran.

Customary law has until now remained characteristic of many less-progressive countries. Where conditions were static for long periods and society remained undisturbed by revolutionary change, the old customs continued to be observed for centuries, not only in primitive areas of Africa but also in Tsarist Russia and pre-revolutionary China. In modern times, however, Western-type codes have tended to be introduced nearly everywhere, not only as a result of subjection to colonial régimes but even in independent countries like Ethiopia. It is hoped that many of the advantages of Western civilisation will come with Western-type laws and that they will be better fitted to regulate a society which plans rapid progress in the future.

Most resistant to change is the law of the family and of succession on death, where intimate personal traditions and religious influences are strong. Some rural customs are also tough in their grounding in local climates and terrains.

The Task of the Courts

In order that law may be enforced, it must be applied to actual situations. It is the task of the court to decide whether certain events have occurred and what the legal consequences of such events are. In modern States courts of law generally enjoy a monopoly of such jurisdiction, but special boards and tribunals which do not follow strict legal procedures are sometimes set up to decide the application of some specialised branch of law, for example, claims to pensions. Laws do not enforce themselves and there is no official in England charged with correcting every breach of law, although some Continental States have an official, the procurator, who has that function. With us the machinery of justice is set in motion on the initiative of civil claimants whose rights have been violated or of victims of crime or their relatives who complain to the police. The interested parties will sooner or later appear before a court or at least have the opportunity of doing so. The decisions of the court will bind all the persons concerned, unless they appeal to a higher court which reverses the first decision.

Trial of Fact

Courts have not always and everywhere been adequately equipped to decide the truth of facts in dispute. In earlier times much reliance was placed on supposed divine signs, like the results of 'judicial duels' fought between two litigants or an accuser and an accused person. Slightly more rational was the weighing of numbers of those willing to swear to their belief in each party's version of events.

In the early days of jury-trial in England a number of local witnesses were summoned to present a pre-agreed report to the court, which was conclusive. Later these jurors came to be used as a group of impartial lay judges to decide other cases, and they were supposed to arrive at the truth on the basis of common sense and experience. It was also reassuring to an accused man that the judge appointed by the King could not by himself condemn the man accused by the Crown. There is little doubt that the use of a jury of twelve has a certain ritualistic significance, but modern jury trial, accompanied by rigorous cross-examination of witnesses by trained lawyers, enjoys general confidence. Of course, all men are fallible, and in recent years attempts have been made to make proof more scientific; we accept fingerprint identifications and the conclusions of handwriting experts, for example. Tape recordings are admitted under strict safeguards, and truth drugs and blood tests may be voluntarily taken.

Legal Rulings

Having determined the true facts as it sees them, the court must give those facts their legal effect. Rules of law may be formulated in various ways. Thus a provision of the criminal law may be embodied in a statute stating that anyone wounding another with intent to injure him seriously may be convicted of a stated offence and sentenced to imprisonment up to some maximum period or a fine of up to a specified amount. In other parts of the law the problem may be more complicated; which of two contestants for ownership of property has the better legal right may depend on the correct analysis of a series of transactions, such as sales or mortgages, spaced over a long period of time, giving each transaction its technical legal effect and working forward on the basis of this transaction to the next one. Legal rulings tend to be bound up in the states of fact to which they are applied and not to embody broad abstract principles.

Court Systems

The methods of organisation of courts, being the product of local history and conditions, tend to vary more widely than the rules of law themselves. In the Middle Ages a welter of different courts existed in Europe; for example, in England there were royal courts, feudal courts, ecclesiastical courts, merchant courts, borough courts and county courts. A feudal court would settle disputes among a lord's vassals and a mercantile court those involving travelling traders; the ecclesiastical courts passed judgment on disputed marriages and the royal courts on major civil disputes. Most European countries in modern times have organised their courts in a geographical pyramid; small civil and criminal cases being decided locally, while higher courts in provincial capitals hear appeals or major disputes, and there is a highest instance in the metropolis. Federal States like the United States of America have separate Federal and State networks of courts, each with separate jurisdictions, and each with a pyramid of courts.

The English judicial system is a mixture of old and new. Civil and criminal courts have remained separate and now follow such different procedures as not to be capable of being united. A proportionately high percentage of civil cases are tried for the first time in the High Court in London. Judges from London tour the country trying civil and criminal cases at Assizes, as in bygone days of poor communications. Small civil cases are tried in local county courts. Petty crimes are tried by lay unpaid magistrates, as in the days of the squirearchy, while crimes of intermediate gravity are tried by magistrates at Quarter Sessions, a system of courts which is now largely professionalised and is no longer strictly linked to the four quarters of the year. Appeals are taken from trial courts to the Civil or Criminal Divisions of the Court of Appeal, and a final appeal may be taken to the House of Lords, which for this purpose consists of judges appointed Law Lords and not of the usual membership of the House.

Civil Procedure

The objective of a civil trial is the same in all countries, but the details differ widely. After preliminary negotiations for a settlement a case is commenced in England by a formal summons served upon the defendant by the plaintiff or someone acting on his behalf. This summons notifies the defendant of the nature of the plaintiff's claim and gives him the opportunity to admit or dispute the claim. If he disputes the claim he must formally contest it on pain of losing the case. There then follows a stage of 'pleadings' designed to isolate the matters in dispute and produce at the end an 'issue' of fact for trial. Pleadings are factual, e.g. 'the defendant failed to pay for the television set specified' followed by the defence 'the television set was defective and unusable'. Matters of law are not pleaded, although they underlie the facts raised by the parties in their pleadings, e.g. a defendant pleads that the set is defective because he is advised that this is a legal answer to a claim for payment for it. The pleadings do not disclose the identity of witnesses or disclose what they will say; such witnesses will only be produced at the trial session of the court. By contrast, German law, for example, requires the parties in their pleadings to name the witnesses they intend to call and to state the relevant legal rules on which they rely, e.g. the numbers of the sections of the German Civil Code which govern the situation in question.

The issue is tried in England in open court. Witnesses are produced to state what happened, and expert witnesses are produced to give conclusions on technical matters (such as the defects in a television set in the above example). Witnesses are generally examined twice, first by the counsel for the party calling them and then ('cross-examination') by the opposing counsel. In some foreign countries witnesses are separately examined out of court and their depositions taken and added to the 'dossier' or official file of the case. English law now allows the parties to the dispute to testify, but in some countries the parties are presumed to be biased in their own favour to such an extent as to be disqualified from testifying.

Trial of civil cases in England is now largely by judge alone, but in the United States juries are still widely used. On the Continent juries are not generally used in civil cases, but in the U.S.S.R. two lay assessors form a court with a trained lawyer as president of the tribunal. Counsel refer to the relevant statutes and case law, and the judge is provided with copies of the authorities on which they rely.

Judgment is usually for a sum of money, and in England and some other countries the winner is reimbursed his legal expenses. If not voluntarily satisfied by the loser, the judgment can be enforced or 'executed' against his assets, or his wages may be attached.

Criminal Procedure

We have seen that in civil cases procedure is straightforward, but the rules of substantive law are very complicated. In criminal cases the opposite is the case. There is seldom any dispute about the definition of the crime which is supposed to have been committed, but the rules of procedure are highly technical and must be strictly complied with, at the risk of the failure of the prosecution case or the reversal of the conviction on appeal to a higher court. Defence counsel, in the interests of his client, will raise every possible objection, and many rules of English criminal procedure are designed to protect the accused.

Criminal proceedings usually begin with the arrest of the accused with or without warrant. Except in petty cases, no trial can proceed unless the accused person is apprehended, though in some foreign countries his trial may be held in his absence. Pleadings are seldom complicated, being generally either a plea of guilty or of not guilty. Conviction follows automatically on the first of these. On not guilty pleaded, on the other hand, a full hearing is required, as in a civil case. The judge in England leaves most of the conduct of the trial to counsel for the prosecution and defence, whereas on the Continent the judge conducts the trial and questions all the witnesses, leaving the lawyers to make the closing speeches.

The jury is still used in England in all serious criminal cases, although the accused often has the option of less formal trial without a jury. The jury deals only with facts, and the judge instructs it on all questions of law and procedure. The judge sums up the case for both sides at the close of the hearing and before the jury arrive at their verdict. On the Continent the lay assessor is equally responsible with the judge for every part of the decision, but generally takes his advice in practice.

Evidence

In many countries any form of proof may be examined by a court if lawfully obtained. In England, however, many types of evidence are excluded altogether or admitted subject to safeguards, where it is feared the lay jury might be unduly prejudiced. As a witness must speak from his own knowledge and submit to cross-examination as to his truthfulness, he is not permitted to repeat statements made to him by other persons ('hearsay'), as such persons should themselves be produced in court for cross-examination. Confessions may only be admitted if freely offered, and even then are not conclusive. Facts which suggest a probability of guilt of the accused but do not directly tend to prove it are also excluded, such as his previous conviction for a similar offence. An attack may always be made on the weight or cogency of such evidence as is admissible, for example, the bias of a witness or his poor powers of recollection or observation.

39

Punishment

The judge alone in England decides the appropriate punishment, but in some countries all members of the court participate: the defence urges arguments in mitigation of sentence after a person is convicted and his background is studied. The punishment must fit the particular criminal as well as the crime.[2]

Suggested Reading

P. S. JAMES, *Introduction to English Law*, Butterworths.
O. H. PHILLIPS, *A First Book of English Law*, Sweet & Maxwell.
H. G. HANBURY, *English Courts of Law*, Home University Library.
G. L. WILLIAMS, *Learning the Law*, Stevens.
A. K. R. KIRALFY, *The English Legal System*, Sweet & Maxwell.

NOTES

[1] See Chapter 4.
[2] See Chapter 7.

4

The Relation of Law
and the Constitution

C. E. P. Davies

'WE ENGLISHMEN,' said Mr. Podsnap to the French gentleman in *Our Mutual Friend*, 'are very proud of our
Constitution, sir. It was bestowed upon us by Providence.
No other country is so favoured as this country.' 'And other
countries,' said the foreign gentleman, 'they do how?' 'They
do, sir,' replied Mr. Podsnap, gravely shaking his head, 'they
do—I am sorry to be obliged to say it—as they do.'

'It was a little peculiar of Providence,' said the foreign
gentleman, laughing, 'for the frontier is not large.'[1]

Mr. Podsnap's enthusiasm may perhaps be forgiven, for
the precise historian Hallam, writing at about the same
time, said much the same thing.[2] And the French gentleman's surprise may be extended, for it is also somewhat
peculiar that Providence did not confer this benefit in a
permanent form, for in England there is no written Constitution, which induced the observation of Tocqueville that
the English Constitution does not exist. If by the Constitution is meant a selection of rules which has been embodied
in one document, or in a few closely related documents[3]
this chapter could be written in the manner of one of the
chapters in a natural history of the world, following a common scheme for all countries. When the contributor came
to Iceland he disposed of the chapter on 'snakes' by saying,
'There are no snakes in Iceland.' But in England the Constitution is the whole system of government,[4] which has

since Norman times had some 900 years of existence and extends back to even remoter origins. During this time great changes have occurred, from feudal to personal monarchy; then a profitable alliance between monarch and Parliament which, however, was replaced by reversion to personal rule without the concurrence of Parliament. This destroyed itself and was eventually replaced by substitution of Crown for monarch and development of the Cabinet system. This at its inception, and for much of the period of its growth, remained subject to control by Parliament, consisting then of Lords and Commons. But gradually the Commons secured domination over the Lords, and many now share the opinion that the Commons may, with development of the modern rigid Party system, have become subservient to the Government. Throughout this period, save for the decade of the Commonwealth, which left surprisingly little mark upon English history, no written constitution has ever proved necessary, nor indeed has there ever been any demand for one, making England in this respect unique among the countries of the world.

Law and Convention

It is, perhaps, because of this that in England particular prominence is given to conventions which, together with rules of law, provide the means by which the State is enabled to achieve its purposes of maintaining peace within and outside its territory, and providing the welfare services which are in modern times accounted one of its main objectives. Conventions are not peculiar to unwritten constitutions; they obtain equally in countries where the constitution is written, as, for example, in the United States of America, where conventions have greatly affected the mode of election of the President and the functions of the Senate, and where the doctrine of 'implied powers' has exercised so much influence.[5] But in England particularly, where there has often been in the past great reluctance to make formal constitutional innovations if informal methods were adequate for the purpose, conventions have special prominence in the constitution. There is need for them because formal rules of law may become unreal as well as rigid unless modified by principles derived from practice. Conventions were called by Mill 'The unwritten maxims of the constitution'[6] but it was Dicey, probably developing an idea originated by Freeman, who first described them as Conventions.[7] These principles have been called by Sir Ivor Jennings 'The flesh which clothes the dry bones of the law', and he also says that they make the legal constitution work and keep it in touch with the growth of ideas.[8] But it would be wrong to regard them only as instruments for making possible the assimilation of new ideas, for they also enable changes to be effected without alteration of the main framework, and thus may take the part of fictions in other parts of the law. Conventions are found in almost every aspect of the complex modern constitution. In the relations between Parliament and the Government, where the principle obtains that the Government is responsible to Parliament, and if defeated in Parliament will either resign or, through the Prime Minister, tender advice to the Crown that Parliament shall be dissolved; in the quite unique respect given in the practice of Parliament to Her Majesty's Opposition; in the composition of the House of Lords when sitting as an appellate court, if indeed this convention has survived the Appellate Jurisdiction Act, 1876; and in the Commonwealth, where the conventions are formulated in the preamble to the Statute of Westminster, 1931, that 'Any alteration in the law touching the Succession to the Throne or the Royal Style and Titles shall hereafter require the assent as well of the Parliaments of all the Dominions as of the United Kingdom' and also that 'No law hereafter made by the Parliament of the United Kingdom shall extend to any of the said Dominions otherwise than at the request and with the consent of that Dominion'.

The form in which most conventions are expressed distinguishes them from more closely formulated rules of law contained in Statutes and judicial decisions, and indeed conventions do not in any way resemble rules of law despite the attempt made by Dicey to establish the doctrine

D

that neglect to observe them would inevitably lead to a breach of the law, at least indirectly. 'The sanction which constrains the boldest political adventurer to obey the fundamental principles of the constitution and the conventions by which these principles are expressed is the fact that the breach of these principles and of these conventions will almost immediately bring the offender into conflict with the courts and the law of the land.'[9] Dicey is, of course, assuming that the convention which is broken has to do with the relation between the Government and the House of Commons, and that a majority in that House requires the convention to be observed, and will therefore sustain it by refusing to pass at least some of the various Acts of Parliament which require annual enactment, thereby making illegal much of the country's administration. But many conventions are not of this kind and, moreover, disregard of a convention may be supported by a majority in the House of Commons; in both these events it would seem that the weapon of refusal to pass the annual Acts would not be available, giving to Dicey's theory only the most limited application. The relation of conventions with the law is more accurately stated by Sir Ivor Jennings, who describes how the courts recognise without enforcing conventions and interpret legislation in the light of their existence.[10] Moreover, there can be no doubt that conventions are habitually observed by all who come within their operation because compliance with them is regarded as the normal constitutional practice and failure to comply would inevitably cause difficulties in the working of the constitution and might bring unpopularity upon the Government.

Consideration of the essential qualities of conventions may be more profitable than comparison with legal rules, though here also there is some lack of precision and it has been said that 'Once having acknowledged the central role of conventions the student of the British Constitution is liable to find that his troubles have only just begun'.[11] For there is no single test which can serve for assignment of principles to this category, and, moreover, the difference between conventions and usages, though crucial, is impossi-

44

ble accurately to define except in the terms used by Sir Kenneth Wheare, who says that 'By convention is meant an obligatory rule; by usage, a rule which is no more than a description of a usual practice which has not yet obtained obligatory force'.[12] Recognition of conventions as obligatory by those who come within their purview is indeed their main characteristic, albeit one difficult if not impossible to apply accurately.

Fundamental Rights

Substantially every modern constitution, most of which are now written, contains prominently some formal declaration of fundamental rights which the Government should secure, or at least not impair. Such declarations often provide an intransigent dilemma for the makers of constitutions, for exclusion of certain principles from this category may alienate some influential body of opinion and result in the constitution being rejected, while inclusion of others may present the equally considerable problem of selecting those to be formulated and providing adequate safeguards against their violation.[13] Commonly included among such principles are, for example, freedom of person and property, of association, of religion, of language, of trade, and even supremacy of law may be thus guaranteed, as in the 'Due Process' clause of the American Constitution.[14] Indeed, there is some obvious affinity between such declarations and the principles of the separation of powers and the rule of law, for all equally endeavour to restrain the power of the Government in the interest of individual freedom. But these guaranteed rights are apt to be illusory, for the wide terms in which they are necessarily expressed may lead to a narrow as well as a broad interpretation, and, moreover, invariably there is added to them a proviso which in some manner warrants their violation if the so-called safety or interests of the State so require. 'No realistic attempt to define the rights of the citizen can fail to include qualifications.'[15]

It is a necessary concomitant of such declarations that

45

they shall not only be formulated in the constitution but also preserved from abolition or amendment; this is normally achieved by some form of 'entrenched clause' in the constitution whereby for their amendment a particular procedure is required differing from the procedure appropriate for enacting other laws, which is also effective for directing general attention to the amendment proposed and for ensuring that it receives popular approval. Such devices include the 'Referendum', by which a proposed amendment is submitted for consideration by the electors of the national assembly, or to bodies of persons different from the legislature; and upon such submissions it is common to require particular majorities, such as two-thirds or even three-quarters. Another device used is to interpolate some period of delay between proposal and enactment of the amendment to enable the country to consider and express a general view about the proposal.

But in the English Constitution there is no such formal declaration of fundamental rights, though it is hoped that they are as freely enjoyed here as in other countries which so declare them. It is, of course, true that Magna Carta, the Bill of Rights (1688), the Act of Settlement (1700), the Acts of Union with Scotland (1706) and with Ireland (1800) and also the Statute of Westminster, 1931, do formulate and establish certain general principles both of personal liberty and of the relationship between different parts of the United Kingdom and the Commonwealth. But many of these principles have been amended by the normal process of legislation, and it is at least open to argument whether they can be considered as entrenched in any formal or indeed informal manner. So at least we are saved from the embarrassment of fundamental rights by the entire informality of their recognition, if indeed they are recognised at all.

The Sovereignty of Parliament

The absence of any formally guaranteed fundamental rights suggests naturally the sovereignty of Parliament. This, and the rule of law and the separation of powers, are generally considered dominant features of the English constitution. This principle means simply that in England each successive Parliament is completely dominant and can repeal or amend any legislation of its predecessors, with the corollary that no Parliament can bind its successors, for to do so would, of course, place restrictions upon them inconsistent with the doctrine. The sovereignty of Parliament in this respect has in the past been generally treated axiomatically and has had little criticism or discussion. 'The power and jurisdiction of Parliament,' wrote Sir Edward Coke, 'is so transcendent and absolute, that it cannot be confined, either for causes or persons, within any bounds.'[16] More simply, it was said by De Lolme that: 'It is a fundamental principle with English lawyers that Parliament can do everything but make a woman a man and a man a woman.'[17] Hitherto this doctrine has been accepted without much discussion and has escaped critical examination. Dicey supported it by instances of the cataclysmic constitutional changes which Parliament has made by the normal process of legislation, such as establishing the succession to the throne by the Act of Settlement, the Acts of Union with Scotland and Ireland, the alteration in the duration of Parliament made by the Septennial Act, 1715, when Parliament extended its own duration from the three years limited by the Triennial Act, 1694, to seven years.[18] And in support of it he added that all these provisions had been later amended by subsequent Parliaments. And to this doctrine is commonly added the by no means inevitable corollary that not only is each successive Parliament supreme but also that no court can question the exercise of its powers save, of course, by interpreting its enactments.[19] But the more critical examination of this principle which has come with development of modern thought suggests a distinction between the area of power of a sovereign legislature and its authority to make procedural rules, with the possibility that in the former sphere Parliament may be supreme but in the latter subject to the existing 'manner and form' prescribed for the time being for legislation.[20] Thus whereas Parliament could undoubtedly repeal the Act of Settlement and the Acts of

47

Union with Scotland and Ireland, it may not be able, save in the prescribed manner, to legislate for Commonwealth Countries[21] or for India or Pakistan,[22] or to deprive Northern Ireland without its consent of its right to inclusion within the Dominions and the United Kingdom.[23]

The Rule of Law

The Rule of Law has been described as 'the natural corollary of the sovereignty of Parliament. The one protected the citizen from arbitrary government, the other from arbitrary justice'.[24] This principle has been used from time to time to convey quite different ideas. The Holy Roman Empire of medieval times was based upon acceptance of a universal ruler of the world. 'The Pope, as God's vicar in matters spiritual, is to lead men to eternal life; the Emperor as vicar in matters temporal, must so control them in their dealings with one another that they may be able to pursue undisturbed the spiritual life and thereby attain the same supreme and common end of everlasting happiness.'[25] The rule of law was at this time the rule of God, the one universal ruler. Later when Grotius had provided, early in the seventeenth century, the intellectual foundation for modern International Law, the same doctrine was used to induce nations to submit to the overriding principles of a law transcending the boundaries of national sovereignty.[26] The doctrine has also been used to emphasise the exceptional character of fundamental rights in constitutions which formulate them and to elevate these to a position above the ordinary and mutable laws of the State. And by development of this idea the same sanctity is claimed for principles which, as in the American constitution, require a particular legislative process for their amendment and are protected by a particular judicial tribunal, and even for the decisions of such tribunal.

But Dicey, who was essentially a common lawyer, gave to the rule of law in England a more precise meaning when he used it to convey the idea, established in the seventeenth century after the bitter constitutional contentions of that

48

time, that the Government should not use the arbitrary power potentially in its hands for the oppression of its subjects. In particular, he insisted that no one should be adversely affected by the Government except for an infringement of the law clearly established in the courts, and also that the courts should be available for everyone who might feel aggrieved by the action of the Government or of anyone else. The rule of law is therefore the supremacy of the courts over the supremacy of the Government or, in modern terms, the denial of any such constraint by the Government as is implied in the conception of a police state. Thus any instance of denial of a remedy in the courts is also an erosion into the rule of law, and every means by which such a denial is frustrated is a means also of preserving the rule or supremacy of law. This principle that all legal relations between the State and individuals shall be determined by legal principles established in the courts must obviously conflict with the other quite legitimate modern idea that these relations should be guided by general and not purely individual considerations, and with the application in public law of the Benthamite principle of the greatest good. Thus application of the rule of law may be involved in every instance where individual liberty, whether in respect of ownership of property, freedom of commerce or of movement, is restricted in the interest of the general public good. Obviously some such restriction may be necessary, and perhaps adherence to the traditional rule of law may be inconsistent with the modern conception of the welfare state. But in the past the law has always been the champion of private rights, and the proper balance may lie in an assessment by, or at least subject to the control of, the courts, which are independent, of the requirements which the State claims as necessary for the fulfilment of its legitimate functions.

The Separation of Powers

The only remaining principle which can be brought into this short outline is the commonly misunderstood doctrine of the Separation of Powers, which also represents an attempt to restrict the power of the State, not only in its administrative but also in the legislative and judicial context. Traces of the doctrine may be found in the *Politics* of Aristotle, but its modern form was originated in John Locke's *Second Treatise on Government*, where he distinguished legislative from judicial power and also discussed the executive power. But the popularity of the doctrine, particularly in America, where it was largely misunderstood, is due to Montesquieu, whose *L'Esprit des lois* was published in 1748. He had studied in England the effect of the Revolution and reached the comfortable conclusion that England was the only country in the world which had made political liberty the direct object of its constitution. He, too, distinguished the legislative from the executive and judicial power, but did not insist upon complete isolation between them, though his writings were erroneously so interpreted by the originators of the American Constitution in 1789. He said no more than that these powers respectively should be separately exercised and not all united in the same authority. 'All would be lost if the same man, or the same body of chief citizens, or the nobility, or the people, exercised these three powers, that of making the laws, that of executing public decisions and that of judging the crimes or the disputes of private persons',[27] though he also insisted that no two of the powers should be exercised wholly by one person. Thus the true doctrine of separation of powers is no more than a requirement that each shall have some control over the others, the doctrine of 'checks and balances' explained and discussed by Bagehot.[28] In England the legislature is controlled by the courts through their interpretation of its enactments; the executive is at least theoretically controlled by the Legislature, for the Government if defeated either resigns or submits to the test of a general election; and the judiciary is controlled by Parliament, which can override its decisions by a Statute.[29] We should do well, however, to ensure that the principle of checks and balances is maintained lest the domination of any one of these powers over the others should bring the disaster which Montesquieu prophesied.

Suggested Reading

L. S. AMERY, *Thoughts on the Constitution*, Oxford University Press.
WALTER BAGEHOT, *The English Constitution*, Fontana.
LORD DENNING, *Freedom under the Law—Hamlyn Lectures*, Stevens.
PROFESSOR R. F. V. HEUSTON, *Essays in Constitutional Law*, Stevens.
SIR IVOR JENNINGS, *The Law & the Constitution*, University of London Press.
SIR IVOR JENNINGS, *The Queen's Government*, Penguin.
LORD LLOYD OF HAMPSTEAD, *The Idea of Law*, Pelican.
LORD MACDERMOTT, *Protection from Power under English Law—Hamlyn Lectures*, Stevens.
MARSHALL & MOODIE, *Some Problems of the Constitution*, Hutchinson.
PROFESSOR HARRY STREET, *Freedom, the Individual and the Law*, Pelican.
SIR KENNETH WHEARE, *Modern Constitutions*, Oxford University Press.

NOTES

[1] Quoted by Sir Kenneth Wheare, *Modern Constitutions*, p. 18, Oxford University Press, 1951.

[2] Hallam, *Middle Ages* (1860), Vol. II, p. 267.

[3] Sir Kenneth Wheare, *Modern Constitutions*, p. 2.

[4] Sir Kenneth Wheare, *Modern Constitutions*, p. 1.

[5] Marriott, *Mechanism of the Modern State*, Vol I, p. 120.

[6] J. S. Mill, 'Representative Government', p. 4, *Works*, Routledge, 1963.

[7] See Sir William Holdsworth, 'The Conventions of the 18th Century Constitution', *17 Iowa Law Review*, p. 161.

[8] Sir Ivor Jennings, *The Law and the Constitution*, 5th ed., 1959, pp. 81 and 82, University of London.

[9] Dicey, *Law of the Constitution*, 9th ed., 1948, pp. 445 and 446, Macmillan, 1961.

[10] Sir Ivor Jennings, *The Law and the Constitution*, pp. 122 *et seq.*

[11] Marshall & Moodie, *Some Problems of the Constitution*, p. 31, Hutchinson, 1961.

[12] Sir Kenneth Wheare, *The Statute of Westminster & Dominion Status*, p. 10, Clarendon Press, 1953.

[13] Sir Kenneth Wheare, *Modern Constitutions*, p. 55.

[14] Judge Learned Hand, *The Bill of Rights*, pp. 31 *et seq.*, Harvard University Press, 1958.

[15] Sir Kenneth Wheare, *Modern Constitutions*, p. 57.

[16] Coke, 4th Institute, p. 36.

[17] Quoted Dicey, *Law of the Constitution*, p. 43, Macmillan, 1961.

[18] Dicey, *Law of the Constitution*, pp. 43 *et seq.*

[19] Cf. Harman, J. in *Hammersmith Borough Council* v. *The Boundary Commission*, *The Times*, 15th December, 1954. S. A. de Smith, 'Bound-

aries between Parliament and the Courts', *Modern Law Review*, Vol. 18, p. 281.

[20] R. F. V. Heuston, *Essays in Constitutional Law*, Chapter 9 *et seq.*, Stevens, 1964.

[21] Statute of Westminster, 1931, s. 4.

[22] Indian Independence Act, 1947, s. 6 (4).

[23] Ireland Act, 1949, s. 1 (2).

[24] C. H. S. Fifoot, *English Law and its Background*, p. 193, George Bell, 1932.

[25] Bryce, *Holy Roman Empire*, pp. 105 and 106, Bailey, 1962. Holdsworth, *History of English Law*, Vol. II, p. 121, Methuen, 1956.

[26] Dicey, *Law of the Constitution*, Introduction to 9th ed. of Professor E. C. S. Wade, p. lxvii.

[27] Montesquieu, *L'Esprit des lois*, Vol. I, p. 220; cited by Sir Ivor Jennings, *The Law and the Constitution*, p. 22.

[28] Bagehot, *The English Constitution*, Chapter VII.

[29] War Damage Act, 1965.

5

Common Law and Equity

A. G. Guest

THE SYSTEMS OF LAW in operation in England, the United States and in most of the Commonwealth are usually known as 'common law' systems. This term—the common law—originally came into use to describe the general law and custom of England, administered by the Royal judges in the King's Courts, as opposed to the different local or particular laws which were in operation in various parts of the country or among special groups of people, such as merchants or clergy. It was a native product, and it owed little or nothing to Roman law ideas which form the basis of many legal systems on the continent of Europe. It was also judge-made law, that is to say, it grew and developed as the result of judicial decisions recorded as precedents by lawyers.

But the words 'common law' are often used in a narrower, more technical sense when they are contrasted with the term 'equity'. It may seem a little surprising, at first sight, that lawyers should draw any distinction between 'law' and 'equity', for the purpose of the law is to do justice, to promote equity. Yet it is common knowledge that the law does not always achieve this aim, and in such a case it can be criticised as leading to an unfair or 'inequitable' result. This is the initial clue to the distinction between common law and equity, for in the fifteenth century the common law of England had become excessively rigid. It was dominated by technicality, encrusted with antiquated procedures and out of harmony with the needs of society. Often, too, it was difficult for a subject without power or influence to obtain redress against wrongs done to him, because bribery, intimidation and armed force were everyday occurrences during that troubled period. He therefore turned for aid to the King's first great officer of state, the Chancellor. This important man was usually an archbishop or bishop with a fine enough conscience and sufficient power to wish to see wrongs righted and good government maintained.

At first the Chancellor merely received petitions addressed to the King or to the King's Council complaining that, for some reason, the petitioner was unable to enforce his rights under the common law. But later he began to make decisions in his own name. His jurisdiction was amorphous and highly personal, so that it was but a short step for him to intervene where the common law—owing to its rigidity —offered no remedy. The decisions which the Chancellor thus made were known as decisions 'in equity'. As he was an ecclesiastic, the Chancellor was prepared to summon the parties before him and examine them as to the state of their 'conscience'—a course from which the common lawyers at that time recoiled. He was particularly concerned with cases of fraud, oppression and breach of confidence. To give but one example, the medieval common-law judges were not prepared to enforce a simple agreement as a contract unless it was recorded in writing under seal, or unless one of the parties had performed his side of the bargain. But as 'keeper of the King's conscience' the Chancellor was prepared to enforce the moral obligation created by a simple promise; he was able to grant relief where the sealed instrument had been lost or destroyed by accident; and he could intervene when the transaction was tainted by fraud or duress.

Initially, the Chancellor's jurisdiction was purely discretionary. 'Equity,' it was said, 'varies with the length of the Chancellor's foot.' But as time went on, he, too, began to adopt the system of precedents in his court. As a result, for several hundred years, two distinct bodies of rules were in existence in the English legal system: the Common Law, administered by the judges in the Courts of King's Bench, Common Pleas and Exchequer; and Equity, administered by the Chancellor in the Court of Chancery. This anomaly is not, however, peculiar to English law, for the distinction between strict and equitable law occurred in other systems, such as Roman law. Indeed, the great jurist and anthropologist, Sir Henry Maine, writing in the late nineteenth century, considered it to be a universal truth that the three devices used to bring strict law into harmony with the needs of society were legal fictions, equity and statute. But in no other legal system was the distinction between law and equity so rigidly maintained.

Relations between the common-law judges and the Chancellor were generally amicable, except for a period beginning in the sixteenth century when the power-hungry tactlessness of Lord Chancellor (Cardinal) Wolsey stirred up illwill between them. This feeling did not wholly subside on Wolsey's downfall, and a running battle was fought—or rather a series of skirmishes occurred—between the courts until the outstanding issues between them were finally settled by the personal intervention of James I. In the meantime, however, the common law had become less rigid and had accustomed itself to change, while equity was beginning to atrophy and develop a rigidity of its own. By 1818 Lord Chancellor Eldon could say, 'Nothing would inflict upon me greater pain, in quitting this place, than the recollection that I had done anything to justify the reproach that the equity of this Court varies like the Chancellor's foot.' To this judge can be attributed many of the evils of the Court of Chancery in the nineteenth century—the delays and expense to litigants so graphically depicted by Dickens in *Bleak House*. In one case he is reported to have said that, 'Having had doubts upon this will for twenty years, there can be no use in taking more time to consider it.' A number of reforms were instituted, but it was not until 1875 that the Courts of common law and the Court of Chancery were merged in one High Court, and Parliament enacted that law and equity should be administered indiscriminately in all courts.

It is sometimes said that law and equity were 'fused' at that time, but this gives rather a false picture. Lawyers still think in terms of common law and equity, although the distinction is much less rigid than it used to be. It is also a mistake to think that, today, the rules of equity are more just and equitable than those of common law. By 'equity', the lawyer normally means those departments of the law, such as trusts, which were previously the domain of the Court of Chancery and which nowadays are usually the subject of the specialist practice of barristers who practise in the Chancery Division of the High Court of Justice.

Common Law

Possibly the most typical examples of common-law cases to-day are those which concern actions relating to contracts and those which arise out of the commission of torts, or civil wrongs. Of course, a common-law practitioner will be concerned with a much wider range of law than these. He will be concerned, for example, with crime and divorce, with disputes arising between landlords and tenants, and to an increasing extent with tribunals and enquiries linked with local authorities and government departments. But his practice is almost bound to include some contract and tort, so that a person who wishes to become a lawyer or study the law will inevitably have to acquaint himself with these subjects.

i. Contract. Most people will be aware what is meant by a contract, and that if a contract is broken the guilty party will be liable in law to pay damages to the other party if he has suffered loss as a result of the breach. Such a simple principle might not seem to hold out any prospect of problems of deep legal complexity. It is true that contracts are often drafted by lawyers in language of considerable technicality—with an archaic ring to the words—so that they are difficult for ordinary citizens to understand. But one might be forgiven for thinking that most problems will arise out of the meaning of the words in the document, and that this is why lawyers are employed: to draft the contract in accurate legal terminology, and to make sure that nothing has been omitted which ought to have been put in. To a certain extent, this popular view is correct, but the problems which arise in the law of contract are more extensive than appear at first sight.

It is a common fallacy, for example, to think that a contract must be in writing in order for it to be binding. But as a general rule this is not so. A contract is just as binding if it is made by word of mouth. Indeed, most of the day-to-day contracts which we enter into are contracts by conduct (as, for instance, when we travel on a bus), or contracts where few words are spoken (as when we buy a tube of toothpaste from a shop). Conversely, many people think that, because a promise is in writing it can be enforced. But this is not always the case. English law takes a very pragmatic view of the idea of a contract. It looks upon a contract as a bargain made between the parties. This aspect of a contract is enforced by the requirement of 'consideration'—a *quid pro quo* for each party's promise. If you undertake to dig my garden for me in return for £5 there is consideration on both sides, for you promise to dig the garden, and I promise to pay you £5. But if this element of reciprocity is lacking —if you simply make me a promise to give me £2 on my birthday—I cannot hold you to it in law, because I have given you nothing and promised you nothing in return. Even if you promise me the £2 in writing, the position is just the same: it is unenforceable. To be binding it must be under seal, which is why, for example, covenants to give money to charities are usually in writing under seal. Once, however, there is consideration the law will not normally enquire whether it is adequate. You can promise to sell me your Rolls-Royce for a shilling, and the law will uphold the transaction.

Most contracts take the form of an offer made by one party and an acceptance by the other. The problems which can arise here can give rise to some very nice questions of law. For example, suppose that I write from Penzance to you in London offering to sell you my car for a certain sum. You sit down and write a letter accepting my offer and post it. Is the contract complete when you write the letter? when you put it in the post-box? when the postman puts it in my letter-box? or when I open and read it? Different legal systems have different answers to this problem, and you can quickly see the difficulties which can arise if the letter is lost or delayed and I get a better offer for my car, or you wish to recall your acceptance. The law has to lay down rules to be applied in such situations, because disputes can arise, and have arisen, where one party will say 'You have contracted with me' and the other will say 'There is no contract here'.

Disputes are especially prone to arise where one of the parties asserts that he only intended to enter into 'a gentlemen's agreement' or that he did not seriously intend that his promise or statement should create any legal relationship. There are, of course, situations where no legal contract is created, like an offer and acceptance of an invitation to tea. But the situation is not always so simple. One of the leading cases in contract law is that of *Carlill* v. *Carbolic Smoke Ball Co.*,[1] where a company issued an advertisement promising to pay £100 to any person 'who contracts the increasing epidemic influenza colds, or any disease caused by taking cold, after having used our smoke ball three times daily for two weeks, according to the printed directions'. It was added that £1,000 was deposited with a certain bank 'showing our sincerity in the matter'. Mrs. Carlill used the smoke ball as directed, but afterwards suffered from influenza and sued the company for the promised reward. Was there any contract to pay the reward? The company contended that it never intended to make a contract by its advertisement, but the Court held that Mrs. Carlill had accepted an offer which was capable of creating a legal obligation and so could claim the £100.

Even if there seems to be a contract, however, there may be reasons why the law should not enforce it. Normally, it is expected that each party should look out for himself—a principle which is sometimes summed up in the Latin maxim *caveat emptor* (let the buyer beware). If one party wishes to protect himself against the existence of facts unknown to him, like the possible presence of dry rot in the timbers of a house, it is up to him to satisfy himself by inspection that such facts do not exist, or to insist upon the incorporation in the contract of special terms by which the other party undertakes liability if defects are present. If he fails to take these precautions he has only himself to blame. It is normally no part of the duty of the seller to point out the defects; he can simply keep quiet and expect the buyer to ascertain them for himself. But this principle does not extend to positive misrepresentations. Suppose that a man wishes to buy a pair of silver candlesticks. He goes to a dealer, who shows him a pair and tells him that they were made in 1741 by the celebrated silversmith, Paul de Lamerie. The man buys them on the strength of this statement, but later discovers that they are in fact modern copies. He will be entitled to have the contract set aside, to return the candlesticks and to recover his money. So if positive misrepresentations are made there is a duty to see that they are accurate. A moralist might say that there was no moral distinction between keeping silent about prejudicial matters which you know to exist and making an actual statement. But the law adopts a more robust attitude and normally holds the seller liable only if he does something positive which misleads the other party. Law is not simply morality, but morality tempered by practical standards of human conduct. So, for example, the law sensibly takes the view that there are some statements that no man with his wits about him would take seriously, like a statement by a house agent that a house is 'a most desirable property' or a soap manufacturer's jingle that its powder 'washes whitest'. If a buyer is so gullible as to take such statements as these at their face value the law is not on his account prepared to shake a moral finger at the inventor of these laudatory 'puffs'.

The law will also refuse to enforce a contract where it has been entered into as the result of threats of physical violence or by the unconscientious use of parental or religious or some other cogent influence, where the parties have contracted under a fundamental mistake, and (in some circumstances) where one of the parties is of unsound mind or under twenty-one years of age and so cannot appreciate the significance of the transaction. It is interesting to consider why the law should intervene in this way. The most

E   59

obvious answer is that it would be unconscientious and inequitable for the law to enforce a contract in these circumstances. But there is also another, more philosophical theory that a contract represents the meeting of the minds, of the wills, of the parties. Each consents to be bound to the other. This consent must be 'true, full and free', so that if there is some impediment, such as fraud or mistake, such consent is lacking and the contract must fail. Few lawyers would subscribe wholeheartedly to this theory today for reasons which it is impossible to detail here. But it is traceable to the idea of 'freedom of contract', whose chief apostles, Adam Smith and John Stuart Mill, saw it as an extension of individual human liberty. Each individual was entitled to promote his own interests by contract, and if he chose to do so he would be bound by his agreement, provided his consent was freely given. Freedom of contract—the freedom to bind oneself by contract—was a cornerstone of liberty in a *laissez-faire* philosophy.

Unfortunately, many of the contracts into which we enter today are not the result of a really free choice. Suppose you take some clothes to the dry-cleaners. You will receive in return a ticket or receipt which will contain the terms upon which the cleaners are prepared to accept your custom. These terms usually take the form of 'exemption clauses' by which the cleaners contract out of liability for loss or damage to the clothes sent for cleaning. You could, of course, attempt to strike out these clauses with a pencil; but then you would not get your clothes cleaned. Or you could take them to another firm of cleaners; but then you would probably encounter the same or a similar set of conditions. The same is true when you take a ticket on a bus or train, or deposit your suitcase in a railway cloakroom. You will be presented (if you care to investigate) with a standard set of conditions which you must accept completely or go without the service you desire. The law, however, still works on the freedom of contract theory: that you are free to accept or refuse to enter the contract if you so wish. Once you do accept, you are bound. This attitude is not entirely consistent with social conditions, but it could be argued that it is a practical one, for the dry-cleaners or bus company could not be expected to enter into an individual contract with each customer. However, the sting lies in the exemption clauses, which may unfairly deprive you of your rights. Contract can therefore be used as an instrument of tyranny—'abuse of contract' in fact. So one of the problems which the law has to face at the moment is to formulate a satisfactory set of principles to protect the consumer against such abuse. One of the most fascinating aspects of the law is to observe how the judges, within the limits set by the fact that they are bound by previous precedents, adapt the law to changing social circumstances.

There is one area of the law of contract in which the courts intervened at an early stage to prevent abuses which might arise. This is in the sphere of illegality. It will be obvious, for example, that the law ought not to enforce a contract whereby two persons agree to commit a murder. There was indeed a case in 1725 where two highwaymen brought an action on a contract to divide the spoils of their excursions; but their solicitors were fined for contempt of court, and both these gentlemen of the road (although this is irrelevant) ultimately met their end upon the gallows. Such gross instances are, however, rare, and the types of illegal contract which have come before the courts are usually of a less spectacular kind. The illegality need not necessarily amount to the commission of a crime. For reasons of public policy the judges have refused to enforce contracts, for example, which promote immorality, which pervert the course of justice or abuse the legal process of the courts, or which affect the freedom or security of marriage. Contracts of this nature are not enforceable in the courts. Moreover, any money paid or property transferred under an illegal contract cannot normally be recovered by legal action. In one case a man paid over £3,000 to the secretary of a charitable organisation in return for a promise of a knighthood. The knighthood never materialised and he sued to get his money back. His action failed because the contract was illegal and he could not invoke the assistance of the court. At the present moment, however, most cases con-

cerning illegality tend to arise out of relatively minor in-
fractions of the criminal law—goods are carried on a vehicle
which does not have the requisite road licence or a ship is
overloaded beyond the 'Plimsoll Line'. If the courts were
simply to refuse to enforce a contract where such an in-
fraction had taken place much injustice might result. So,
again, the judges have had to modify the law in order to
keep up with modern social conditions, and to decide when
they will, and when they will not, enforce a contract with an
illegal element.

The usual remedy for breach of contract is damages. In
very many contract cases there will be no doubt that a
contract has been entered into and that it has been broken,
but the dispute between the parties will turn on how much
money can be recovered as damages by one party from the
other. The general object of damages for breach of contract
is to put the injured party in the same position, from a
financial point of view, as he would have been if the contract had been performed and not broken. But damages
will be awarded only in respect of loss actually suffered by
the injured party. Breach of contract is not a crime, so that
the courts cannot 'fine' the party in default, nor can they
award damages to mark disapproval of his conduct. If the
injured party has suffered no loss as the result of the breach
he cannot claim any substantial compensation. In some
systems of law it is possible to include a term in a contract
whereby one party promises to pay the other a definite sum
by way of penalty for breach of contract. But in England the
courts will not allow such a practice and will give damages
only in respect of the loss actually suffered. Cases imple-
menting this rule have arisen recently in relation to hire-
purchase agreements. Finance companies which let goods on
hire-purchase frequently stipulated that, if the hirer de-
faulted before he had paid all the instalments, the company
was to be entitled to take back the goods, keep the instalments already paid and recover from the hirer a fixed proportion—say 75%—of the hire-purchase price. These
oppressive clauses have, however, now been struck down by
the courts, which have held that provisions which require

the hirer to pay a fixed sum are normally to be regarded as imposing a penalty. So the finance company can only recover the loss (if any) which it has actually suffered. Decisions like these obviously have a most far-reaching effect upon the common institutions of modern social life and the financial situation of persons who use hire-purchase as a means of buying articles for their homes.

Contract, in fact, regulates not only the day-to-day life of individuals but also the whole commercial and industrial life of the community. It is far from being an ivory-tower exercise, since the rulings of the judges can have profound effects on economics and trade. As a result, the law of contract is studied not only by those who wish to become professional lawyers but also by accountants, bankers, company secretaries and persons engaged in commerce and industry.

ii. Torts. The concept of a tort, or civil wrong, requires some initial explanation. Every legal system must make provision for the compensation of persons who suffer damage or who are injured by the wrongful acts of others. This is quite distinct from the criminal law. The criminal law exists to protect society as a whole from acts which are particularly harmful to the community. A wrongdoer, if convicted of a crime, will be liable to a penalty—such as a fine or imprisonment—inflicted by the State. A criminal prosecution is not designed to give redress to the person injured by compelling the wrongdoer to pay for the damage he has done. This is the province of the law of torts. Also the criminal law is concerned to punish a relatively narrow range of anti-social acts where the criminal normally has *mens rea*—a wicked intention to break the law. The law of torts, however, is concerned with a much wider range of injurious actions which do not necessarily amount to criminal offences and where the damage caused may be accidental, that is to say, unintended by the wrongdoer. For example, if you go to visit a block of flats and are injured when the lift falls down the lift shaft owing to a defect in the machinery, no criminal offence will probably have been committed for which the person responsible for maintaining the lift could be punished. But you will be entitled to claim compensation from him by an action in tort if he can be shown to have been negligent.

Many legal systems contain very general provisions which confer a right of action on a person injured in this way. The French Civil Code, for instance, states that, 'Every act of a person whatsoever, which causes damage to another, places that person by whose fault it has occurred under an obligation to pay compensation for the damage'. For historical reasons, however, English law does not adopt such a general approach. It consists of a number of individual torts designed to afford protection for personal or proprietary interests against certain types of conduct. Thus the tort of libel protects the interest which a man has in his reputation against false statements in writing made by others. And the intentional interference with a man's land, or goods, or person is protected by the tort of trespass. At one time there was a separate writ or summons for each of the many separate torts, so that the law of torts was described as 'chaos with a full index'. But these procedural niceties have now been swept away, and more definite patterns are beginning to emerge.

The most general basis of liability in tort is that of negligence. If I negligently injure you, say, in a collision between our two motor-cars, I will be liable to pay you damages for the injury which you have sustained. Somewhat surprisingly, it was not until 1932 that it could be said to be a general principle of English law that a person who had suffered loss or damage as the result of another's negligence was entitled to be compensated. But in that year a case arose which is familiar to all lawyers as the 'snail in the bottle' case: *Donoghue* v. *Stevenson*.[2] A woman went with a friend to a café in Paisley and there ordered a bottle of ginger beer. The bottle was made of dark opaque glass, and there was no reason to suspect that anything was wrong with the contents. The café proprietor poured out some of the ginger beer into a tumbler and the woman drank it. Her friend then poured out the rest, and the remains of a snail—in an advanced state of decomposition—fell into the tumbler. As a result of the nauseating sight, the woman suffered shock and, what is worse, contracted gastro-enteritis in consequence of the impurities in the ginger beer. She sued the manufacturers of the ginger beer for damages for negligence. Now there was a long line of cases which established that there was no liability on the part of the manufacturer of a product to the ultimate consumer in the absence of a direct contractual relationship. But the woman had no contract with the manufacturer; she had purchased the ginger beer from the café proprietor, and her contract (a contract of sale) was with him. So the manufacturers contended that they were not liable. But the House of Lords held that a person was generally liable to compensate persons whom he could reasonably foresee might be injured as a result of his negligent act, and the woman recovered damages for the injury which she suffered.

In the course of his judgment, Lord Atkin said: 'You must take reasonable care to avoid acts or omissions which you can reasonably foresee would be likely to injure your neighbour.' This might seem to be a salutary and sensible principle; but it cannot always be applied without qualification. Suppose that I am the proprietor of a greengrocer's shop. You come and open up another greengrocer's shop in the vicinity. You can reasonably foresee that your act will be likely to injure my business. But it would be strange if the law were to hold you liable to me in damages for fair trade competition. Again there may be a difference of opinion about liability for omissions to act. If I am drowning in a river, should the law hold you liable in damages to my widow and children if you fail to dive in and pull me out? A number of situations will undoubtedly occur where it may be unwise for the law to apply without qualification the principle embodied in Lord Atkin's statement. So lawyers have to try to analyse and even to anticipate such situations; they have to attempt to formulate rules based upon the social values and attitudes prevalent in the community; and they have to try fairly to distribute the losses which inevitably occur as a result of living together.

In some circumstances English law takes the view that a

person should be placed under strict liability for his acts, that is to say, he should have to pay damages to anyone injured, even though he was not guilty of any fault. Some activities may be so dangerous—so 'ultra-hazardous'—that anyone who embarks on them will be considered to do so at his peril. One instance of strict liability occurs in the case of dangerous animals. If the owner of a stately home decides to keep a number of lions in order to attract visitors, he will be liable to anyone injured as the result of their escape, regardless of whether he was negligent or not. Indeed, it could almost be said to be a general principle that any dangerous activity attended by exceptional risk will attract strict liability. This was the basis of the leading case of *Rylands* v. *Fletcher*, decided in 1866, where a mill-owner decided to construct a large reservoir on his land for the purpose of bringing water to his factory. On the site of the reservoir there was a disused and blocked-up mine shaft—a fact which escaped the notice of the contractors whom he employed to construct the reservoir. When the reservoir was filled with water, the water flowed down into the shaft and flooded a neighbouring mine. The House of Lords held that, although the mill-owner himself was guilty of no negligence, he had for his own purposes brought on his land a large quantity of water and thus created an inherently dangerous situation. He was therefore bound to keep it in at his peril, and, since he had not done so, was liable for the consequences of its escape.

Strict liability may be justified on the ground that, if one of two persons have to suffer as the result of the dangerous situation, it ought to be the person who created the danger rather than the one who was injured as a result. But it is a somewhat exceptional principle in English law. The feeling that there should be 'no liability without fault' is deeply rooted in the law of torts—as indeed it may be in popular morality—so that the principle has mainly been confined to activities which create extraordinary risks to others, either in the magnitude of the danger or in the high probability of its occurrence. One of the tasks of the law is to decide, in a given situation, whether strict liability is justified or not.

At present, for example, the law does not impose strict liability upon the drivers of motor-cars; they are liable only if negligence is proved. It could be argued that driving a motor-car is just as hazardous as building a reservoir. But does it create a risk which could be termed 'extraordinary' in a modern society? Value judgments like these crop up constantly in the law of torts and make the subject one of absorbing social interest. Such value judgments are even present in deciding a question of negligence, for the standard of care required of a motor-car driver is that of a *reasonable* man. The particular driver may be suffering from nervous anxiety because his wife has left him, or have had too much to eat or drink, or he may just not be skilful at driving a car. But the law will hold him liable if he has failed to exercise such care as a reasonable man would employ in the circumstances.

As might be expected, the main object of the law of torts is to compensate persons in respect of bodily injury or damage to their property. But in a modern society people also look to the law to protect them against purely financial loss. Obviously, different considerations must be taken into account when considering this type of problem. It is one thing to award me compensation when I have my leg broken in a motor accident due to the negligence of another, but quite another thing to give a similar right of action against the wrongdoer to my business partner, who may have suffered financial loss as a result of my being in hospital. Where purely financial loss is concerned, the general tendency of the law is to insist that it should have been deliberately inflicted by the wrongdoer. Mere negligence is not enough. If it were, the financial consequences of a slight accident might be infinite. In this sphere, too, the law has to consider very carefully the type of conduct which has brought about that loss. A businessman, for example, expects to be protected against unfair trade competition. But what types of trade competition are unfair? In the rough and tumble of commercial and industrial relations the law has to mark out a very precise and difficult path between those practices which may be considered legitimate and those which may not. In a recent case, certain officials of a trade union threatened to call their men out on strike in breach of their contracts of employment unless an employer dismissed one of his employees who would not join the union. There is nothing illegal about a 'closed shop' policy, and the sole question was whether the means employed to achieve this object were legitimate or not. You can see that the decision which the courts had to make in this case was of immense importance in the sphere of labour relations.

A writer on the law of torts has very truly pointed out that no simple and all-embracing formulas can be offered as solutions in this branch of the law, because the problems which arise in tort litigation are manifold and often complex. It is for this reason that the topic is of great interest for both students and practitioners.

Equity

To many lawyers, an 'equity practice' is roughly equated with that type of legal work which is undertaken by those barristers who practise in the Chancery Division of the High Court. Its Mecca is the mellow brick buildings and green fields of Lincoln's Inn. Chancery barristers are mainly concerned with transactions concerning property and land—with conveyances, mortgages, leases, wills and trusts. Their work is chiefly 'paper work', that is to say, they are concerned with the drafting and perusal of documents, and in giving advice on property matters. They are very much less often in court than a common-law barrister, and so the atmosphere in Lincoln's Inn is more like that of the academic atmosphere of a University.

But in a narrower sense the term 'equity' means those rules administered by the Court of Chancery before the reforms of the nineteenth century. One cannot attempt to give here an extensive account of all the branches of equity. But one topic may be considered as essential to the idea of equity—the law of trusts.

It is extremely difficult to give an accurate definition of the concept of a trust, but in rough-and-ready language a trust exists where a certain person or persons (known as trustees) hold money or other property on behalf of another person or persons (known as the beneficiaries). Trusts were peculiarly the domain of the Court of Chancery because of the confidence which was reposed in the trustees to see that the objects of the trust were carried out. It would be inequitable if the trustees could simply put the money or property into their own pockets. And a person who created a trust, say, a man who made a will, would usually lay down certain conditions as to how the trust fund was to be administered, and he expected the trustees to observe these conditions. Trusts were (and still are) used to make provision for the children of a family, especially when the children are young and cannot be expected to manage their own affairs. A certain type of trust—the charitable trust— has from very early times also been used to provide a means by which funds devoted to charitable objects could be properly administered. There are today in existence thousands of charitable trusts. Some of them are large and some of them very small, but in the aggregate their trustees administer funds totalling many millions of pounds. In these modern days of high taxation, however, one of the most important aspects of trust law is the opportunity which it legitimately provides to a man so to arrange his financial affairs as to reduce the amount payable to the Inland Revenue by way of income tax, capital gains tax and death duties.

The law of trusts has undergone a considerable change in recent years. At one time trusts were extremely tightly drawn. A person, for example, might wish to arrange for his property to be tied up in his family after his death. The trust deed would prescribe very minutely how the various interests of the beneficiaries were to be apportioned and in what shares; and it might state what was to happen to those interests when a beneficiary died. In this way the person creating the trust could settle his property on his children and, after their death, on his grandchildren and so on within the limits allowed by the law. But such a practice meant that death duties had to be paid each time a beneficiary died, so that the bulk of the trust fund found its way into the hands of the Government. As a result, modern trusts are much more loosely drawn. They give the trustees wide powers to administer the fund as they, in their discretion, think fit. Much of the old law on the devolution of interests and the rights and duties of trustees has therefore become of little practical importance. Lawyers are now concerned with the way trusts can be employed in practice, although the rules relating to charitable trusts are still of considerable significance.

From the point of view of a solicitor, the branch of equity which he encounters most frequently is that concerning succession to the property of persons who have died. At one time the administration of the estates of deceased persons was the prerogative of the ecclesiastical courts, but the Court of Chancery took over this jurisdiction as the ecclesiastical courts declined in power. Every solicitor is required to be familiar with the rules of succession, and with the rights and duties of executors and administrators, and to many this branch of the law will form a substantial part of their everyday work.

Statute

So far, in this chapter, the impression may have been conveyed that all the law which is likely to be encountered is the product of, and enshrined in, the decisions of the judges in the courts. This is emphatically not the case, for increasingly the law is to be found in statutes enacted by Parliament. The legislature has intervened very considerably in both the law of contract and the law of torts—in most cases to reform the judge-made law or to bring it into harmony with modern social conditions. Great social statutes, such as the Rent Acts and the National Insurance Acts, have also been passed, and a constant stream of social legislation flows out from Parliament each year. In 1965, for example, eighty-three new statutes found their way on to the Statute Book, one of which (the Finance Act) had ninety-five sections and twenty-two schedules. There are also a great mass of Orders and Regulations issued by Government Departments. From a practical point of view, the chief task of the lawyer might well be said to be the exacting one of finding the relevant statutory law on a given point. On a higher plane, however, he will be concerned with the meaning and interpretation of the words of the enactment. Words are the tools of a lawyer, but nowhere does the question of semantics assume greater importance than in the interpretation of statutes.

Unfortunately there is a limit to human precision and perspicacity, and the Parliamentary draftsman has been said—somewhat unfairly—to be the cause of half the litigation in this country. Certainly the provisions of statutes are frequently obscure. On one occasion a celebrated judge pointed out that he had read a section of a certain statute hundreds of times, but continued: 'Despite this iteration I must confess that, reading it through once again, I have very little notion of what the section is intended to convey, and particularly the sentence of two hundred and fifty-three words, as I make them, which constitutes sub-section 1. I doubt if the entire statute book could be successfully searched for a sentence of equal length which is of more fuliginous obscurity.' You may well be one of those to whom the prospect of unravelling complicated semantic crossword puzzles will prove an exciting intellectual exercise, but to most lawyers the problems of statutory interpretation are simply regarded as crosses which they needs must bear with equanimity.

Suggested Reading

P. S. ATIYAH, *An Introduction to the Law of Contract*, Clarendon Press.
J. G. FLEMING, *An Introduction to the Law of Torts*, Clarendon Press.
W. GELDART, *Elements of English Law*, Oxford University Press.
A. L. GOODHART, *English Law and the Moral Law*, Stevens.

NOTES

[1] [1893] 1 Q.B., 256.
[2] [1932] A.C., 562.

6

Commercial Law

(A) SALE OF GOODS

A. D. Hughes

'COMMERCIAL LAW' is a term that covers a great many branches of the law having for practical purposes only two features in common. In the first place, at the root of nearly all of them lies the concept of contractual obligation—that is to say, an obligation enforced by the law because the party charged with it has expressed his agreement to perform it. In comparatively few instances will the obligations of the parties be entirely, or even largely, the product of a conscious hammering out of an express agreement, for in many cases this process would either be unnecessary or even impossible. The language, and consequently the effect, of insurance contracts is stereotyped, and the same is true of contracts for the carriage of goods, especially by sea. Contracts for the sale of goods will usually contain an elaborate series of undertakings by the seller, by virtue of the 'implied' terms contained in the Sale of Goods Act, 1893, even though the actual agreement between the parties contains no reference to these undertakings at all.

In other cases the basically contractual nature of the obligations has been somewhat obscured by the refinements of modern commercial practice. A block of shares in a company, for instance, is, in theory, merely a symbol of the rights under the contract made when the shares were first allotted, but it is usual, and quite proper, to think of shares as being a kind of property, and not just a contract. The position of negotiable instruments is similar. A negotiable instrument is a document, usually a promise or order to pay a sum of money, which is transferable by delivery and has the legal quality of conferring full title on the transferee who takes in good faith and for value, even though the transferor had no title, because, for example, he had stolen it from the true owner. It is this last quality which distinguishes a 'negotiable' document from instruments that are not negotiable; whether a particular type of instrument is negotiable or not depends ultimately on whether it is customarily treated as negotiable by the merchants who make use of it. The commonest types of negotiable instrument encountered in everyday life are banknotes, cheques and promissory notes. Whether the affinity with contract is strong, as in the case of a promissory note, or weak, as in the case of a cheque, negotiable instruments are treated in practice as the equivalent of the *money*, not of the right to claim the money.

The second common feature of the fields of law we are now considering is the obvious, and more practical, one that they are all of particular importance in business transactions. This is not to say that they only apply to business transactions—far from it. English law makes no distinction in principle between the contracts of a businessman and those of any other person. The collective term 'Commercial Law' merely expresses the simple fact that certain transactions form an indispensable part of business life, and are engaged in somewhat less frequently, and in some cases hardly at all, by the ordinary man in the street.

It was clearly impossible, in a work of this nature, to give even the most superficial account of everything that could with justification be regarded as part of Commercial Law. We felt rather that it would be of greater value to select a small number of topics and attempt to explain the leading features of these as fully as possible. Accordingly, we have limited the discussion which follows to three subjects: sale of goods, agency, and companies and partnership.

It is not, unfortunately, possible to talk of the 'law of sale' in England because we have in fact three types of sales law, which differ considerably from one another. There is one set of rules for land, another for 'intangible' property (for example, debts, shares, patents, copyrights) and a third set for moveable goods. As the name indicates, the law of sale of goods is limited to the case of moveable property.

Here the element of contractual obligation comes very much to the fore. The duties of buyer and seller and the effects of the contract are determined almost exclusively by the agreement between the parties, as supplemented by the implied terms of the Sale of Goods Act. The making of a contract of sale is a very simple matter indeed. Except in the case of certain consumer credit transactions, no writing is necessary, and countless contracts of sale are concluded and performed every day without the slightest formality being observed, in many cases without even a word being spoken. All that is required is that the parties should demonstrate, by words or actions, their willingness to buy and sell respectively, and that the goods should be identified (prior agreement on the price is usual, but not essential in all cases). In a supermarket, for instance, the display of the goods, selection by the customer, presentation to the cashier and acceptance by the latter satisfy all the requirements for a contract of sale to come into existence.

In such a case most of the obligations undertaken by the parties are determined for them by the Sale of Goods Act, and their scope is relatively certain. But this is not always so: in a transaction such as the sale of a used car by a dealer it may be a very difficult matter to decide exactly what obligations the seller undertook. Not everything that passes his lips in the attempt to make a sale will be treated as a serious undertaking having contractual force. (We are not here concerned with actual fraud, for example, deliber-ately falsifying the mileage reading. If it can be proved, fraud is always actionable, whether the statement was part of the contract or not. The trouble is that fraud is much more easily suspected than proved.) This area of the law bristles with distinctions whose only merit is that they give the Court much greater room for manoeuvre than it normally has and allow it to reach decisions in accordance with the merits of the case without the hindrance of settled legal principles.

Leaving aside such vague statements as 'outstanding value' which are unlikely to be taken as more than sales talk and thus create no obligation of any kind, the primary distinction is between a statement which constitutes a term of the contract and one which induces the making of the contract but does not form part of it. The latter is known as a 'mere representation' (or 'misrepresentation' if the falsity of the statement is being emphasised), and the buyer's only remedy for a mere representation is a limited right to rescind the contract. (By rescinding a contract we mean putting the parties back to the position they had before the contract was made: the buyer returns the goods, the seller returns the money and the mutual contractual obligations are cancelled out.) The exact extent of the right to rescind is a matter of considerable doubt, but it is quite clear that if, as usually happens, the buyer does not discover the falsity of the statement until after he has paid for and taken delivery of the car the chances of his being held entitled to rescind the contract are not good. He cannot recover damages at all (fraud apart).

On the other hand, if the statement *is* a term of the contract the buyer is in a much better position. He may claim damages in any case, and has in addition an effective right to rescind the contract in most instances. It will be obvious, therefore, that some workable criterion is desirable for making the distinction between mere representations and terms of the contract, but this has in the past been conspicuously lacking. The traditional test was 'the intention of the parties' (as evidenced by their words, actions and the surrounding circumstances). Recently a distinguished judge has given this test a more concrete form by emphasising the part that the presence or absence of fault in the maker of the statement should play. If a dealer makes a statement about the past history of the car which he should have known might be inaccurate, and which he could easily have checked, he is at fault should the statement prove to be incorrect, and the statement will be regarded as a term of the contract. This is a great advance on the previous law, but even so, the circumstances of the particular case (including, to some extent, the merits and demerits of the parties) will continue to play a decisive role.

Where the statement by the seller is held to be a term of the contract, the possible remedies for the buyer again depend, partly at any rate, on a rather elusive distinction, namely that between warranties and conditions. Both words are used in a special sense in the Sale of Goods Act. For practical purposes it may be said that a warranty is a minor, or lesser, term of the contract ('collateral to the main purpose of the contract' is the phrase used in the Act) and a condition is a major term. In theory the intention of the parties decides what is of minor and what of major significance, but the tendency is to treat very nearly all points of agreement as conditions of the contract, and it may be noted that of the terms implied in a contract of sale under the provisions of the Act, only two (very unimportant) terms are warranties.

For breach of condition, as opposed to breach of warranty, the buyer is given the right to reject the goods—leaving the seller, incidentally, to bear the cost of collecting them from the agreed place of delivery—and have his money back, in addition to a possible claim for damages. This is a very drastic remedy, and is, indeed, as severe as that for fraudulent misrepresentation, but available even though the seller may have acted in perfect good faith. If the seller has not yet been paid, he is put in a very awkward position by a buyer's claim to reject for breach of condition. However, a number of factors help to maintain a balance between the parties and prevent rash claims to reject. In export transactions at least, where the risk for the seller is greatest, modern financing methods enable him to obtain payment before any dispute can arise. Further, a buyer must always weigh the advantage of the right to reject against the disadvantage of losing the seller's goodwill. Finally, the Sale of Goods Act itself imposes several qualifications on the right to reject.

Some of the statutory qualifications would, if applied literally, deprive the right to reject of all force. Partly to avoid this result, yet another distinction has been drawn by the courts in classifying the terms of the contract. A category of 'super-conditions' has been created, known today as fundamental terms, breach of which constitutes a fundamental breach. The doctrine of fundamental breach has received particular attention in recent years in connection with hire-purchase contracts, but the principle, if not the name, has long been well known in the law of sale.

The idea is quite simple: if A says to B, 'I will *sell* you *my Austin Mini*' at such and such a price, and B accepts, the use of the word 'sell' obliges A to transfer ownership in the car to B, and the use of the words 'Austin Mini' constitutes a guarantee that the car *is* an Austin Mini. Both these obligations are 'fundamental' in that they follow inescapably from the words used, and if either one is not fulfilled A has *completely* failed to perform the contract. If the car does not belong to A, or if it is not an Austin Mini, B is in the same position as if he had never received a car at all, and nothing (except his own conduct in subsequently parting with possession of the car or electing to keep it with knowledge of the breach on A's part) can deprive B of his right to reject.

Whether A is the owner of the car is a simple matter to decide, but whether the car is an Austin Mini is not such a straightforward question as it might seem. Obviously a Fiat is not a Mini, but suppose that when A delivers the Mini it will not go. Is it still an Austin Mini? The Courts have wrestled with this poser on a number of occasions, and they have come down in favour of the view that a contract for the sale of a machine, such as a car, means *a machine that will work*. Just how well it must work will depend on circumstances of age, price, apparent condition and so on.

Probably the greatest impetus to the development of the idea of fundamental terms was given by the common practice of inserting blanket 'exemption clauses' into sales contracts. An exemption (or 'exclusion') clause is one which states that all warranties and conditions of any kind are excluded from the contract. Such a clause provides complete protection for the seller against implied terms which are not fundamental, but does not avail him where fundamental terms are concerned. The only means of escape from the fundamental terms is to avoid using the words (or actions) which would give rise to the implication of the term in the first place. An extreme example would be where the 'seller' says, 'I agree to transfer to you whatever interest I may have in this object. I believe it to be an Austin Mini, but I cannot guarantee that.' Provided the 'seller' does transfer his whole interest in the object, the buyer cannot complain; the contract has been completely performed, even though the object is not what the buyer thought it was, and he has not become owner of it.

Several references have already been made to the implied terms set out in the Sale of Goods Act, and we must now consider these in more detail. The classification of terms into warranties, conditions and fundamental terms can be adopted here, too, though the Act itself uses only the two-fold division of warranties and conditions. To start at the top, with fundamental terms, there is, first, an implied condition that the seller has the right to sell the goods. This obliges the seller to transfer ownership to the buyer, and is, as we have seen, inherent in the idea of 'selling'. The transfer of ownership, also referred to as the 'passing of property' in the goods to the buyer, must not be confused with delivery, in the sense of handing the goods over to the buyer. (The distinction between ownership and possession is considered later, in chapter 9.) Ownership, or property, is transferred as and when the parties agree that it shall be transferred, and the goods need never leave the seller's possession for property to pass. If no express agreement has been made on this point the parties are presumed to have intended that property shall pass, in the case of specific, identified goods, as soon as the contract is concluded. The chief importance of the passing of property is that the goods, whether paid for or not, are then presumed to be 'at the buyer's risk'; that is, the buyer must bear any loss arising from damage to or destruction of the goods, unless the loss was caused by the fault of the seller. But this presumption also gives way to any express agreement on the point.

Secondly, it is the seller's duty to deliver the goods. This statement is, however, a little misleading, because the seller is not obliged to bring the goods to the buyer unless he has *expressly* agreed to do so. All that delivery means is giving up possession of the goods to the buyer, and it is *prima facie* the buyer's duty to *collect* the goods from the seller.

Thirdly, where goods are sold by description there is an implied (fundamental) condition that the goods shall correspond with the description. This is the same case as that of the Austin Mini, discussed earlier. In that example the parties agreed about a specific car, but there is nothing to prevent the making of a contract of sale where the parties have no particular object in mind, but merely agree on the kind of goods to be sold, as when a new car of a particular model is ordered from a dealer. In all cases the principle is the same: the seller must supply *exactly* the kind of goods which the buyer agreed to take.

Fourthly, where goods are sold by quantity (such as grain or coal) the seller must supply *exactly* the right quantity, for the buyer is entitled to refuse a tender of the wrong quantity, whether it is of too much or too little. The seller will be permitted to deviate from the agreed quantity only where the variation is microscopic, and for that reason it is usual to have an agreed 'margin': the order will be for '1000 tons, 3% more or less', but the seller must still keep within the margin.

Turning now to the non-fundamental conditions implied by the Act, we find that there are two, both serving much the same purpose. The Act departs from the ancient principle of *caveat emptor* (which implies that if the buyer wants any guarantee of the quality of the goods he must stipulate for it expressly) by providing that in certain cases the seller is taken to guarantee the quality of the goods.

If the seller is a dealer in the kind of goods in question, then, *subject to contrary agreement,* there are implied conditions that the goods are fit for the purpose for which they are required and that they are of 'merchantable' quality.

The condition of fitness for purpose only arises, according to the Act, when the buyer makes known to the seller the purpose for which he requires the goods, in such a way as to show that he is relying on the seller's skill and judgment. The intention appears to have been to limit the implied condition to cases where the buyer wanted an assurance of the *suitability* of the goods for some special purpose, rather than an assurance of their quality in general. However that may be, the courts have consistently applied the condition of fitness for purpose where only the quality of the goods was in issue, with the result that there is in practice a considerable overlap between this condition and the condition of merchantable quality. There *are* differences between the two, but they are somewhat illogical, and almost accidental at the present day, and need not concern us.

The Act also sets out two implied warranties relating to the question of title, but they are so rarely applied that we need not pursue the matter further.

Little need be said about the obligations of the buyer. He must pay the price and take delivery of the goods, but, of course, agreements for delivery prior to payment in full are commonplace.

The Sale of Goods Act is remarkable for the wealth of remedies which it puts at the parties' disposal. We have already pointed out that the buyer may reject the tendered performance if the seller is in breach of a condition (a rather circumscribed right if the condition is not fundamental), and may also recover damages for a breach of any term of the contract. It should be noted, however, that many breaches by the seller will cause no real financial loss to the buyer. If the seller is unable to deliver the goods ordered, but the same goods are readily available elsewhere at the same, or a lower price, the buyer's proper course is to obtain the goods from the alternative source, and his right of action against the original seller will only be for nominal damages. On the other hand, there may be real loss to the buyer for which he can recover nothing, for the principle is that compensation will only be given for loss that the seller could have been expected to anticipate as a result of his breach.

Thus, if a manufacturer fails to deliver a piece of machinery ordered for a factory with the result that production is held up, wages have to be paid to idle workers, and contracts and goodwill are lost, the loss to the factory may be enormous. But if the manufacturer had no reason to know that such consequences would follow, his liability would not extend beyond the increased cost of obtaining a substitute machine, and an estimated amount for the loss of 'normal' profits during the period of delay.

In rare cases the buyer may obtain a decree of specific performance, that is, an order that the defaulting seller shall perform the contract as agreed instead of paying damages for non-performance. Specific performance is a discretionary remedy, not one the buyer can claim as of right, and it is settled that the discretion will not be exercised in the buyer's favour unless the article sold is something unique.

The remedies available to the seller are even more complex. If the goods have been delivered, but not paid for, the seller can recover the amount of the price. If the buyer fails to take delivery the seller may sue for the price if the property in the goods has passed to the buyer, or if the price was payable 'on a day certain irrespective of delivery'; otherwise he has an action for damages, and has a right to withhold delivery (in some circumstances referred to as a 'lien' on the goods) until the price is paid. Although the same general principles govern both the seller's and the buyer's right to damages, certain practical differences appear. In normal market conditions, for example, a retailer will be able to claim his loss of profit from a defaulting customer, even though he disposes of the goods to someone else at the same price, for no special knowledge is required on the part of the customer to realise that without the default the seller could have made two sales, and hence had twice the amount of profit.

(B) AGENCY

A. D. Hughes

THE LAW OF AGENCY governs the relationships which arise when one person performs some legally significant act—typically the making of a contract or a disposition of property—on behalf of another person. Such situations are usually extremely complex, for they may involve three distinct pairs of relationships. First, there are the mutual rights and obligations of the person on whose behalf the act was done (the principal) and the person performing the act (the agent). Agency, in this aspect, is a 'fiduciary' relationship (that is, a relationship of trust), and the agent must often subordinate his own interests to those of the principal. For example, if the agent uses his position or confidential knowledge of the principal's affairs to obtain an advantage for himself he must account to the principal for the advantage. Secondly there is the relationship between the agent and the person with whom he dealt on the principal's behalf (usually called, simply, 'the third party'). This is the least important of the three relationships, and normally comes into play only when things go wrong. Finally, the law has to consider the effect of the agent's act as between the principal and the third party.

The principal–third-party relationship is the centre-piece of the law of agency, for it is the practical expression of the primary object of this branch of the law, namely, to secure that transactions made by an agent are as effective as they would have been if the principal had dealt in person with the third party. The ability to 'act' without being physically present is often an advantage, and in many cases an absolute necessity. A corporation, such as a limited company registered under the Companies Act, could not function at all without the law of agency. As is explained below, the corporation is a 'person' in the eyes of the law, an entity completely distinct from its members and officers, but every decision of the corporation has to be taken *on its behalf* by someone else.

The business corporation is a principal with many agents. We also find agents with many principals: brokers, auctioneers and, to a lesser extent, solicitors form a class of professional agents. Ironically, most of the people who actually call themselves 'agents', are not performing functions which are those of an agent in law, or not to any substantial degree. The travel agent, for example, is really no more an agent of the airline or shipping company than the grocer is an agent of the firm whose canned vegetables he sells. Even the estate agent receives his commission, for the most part, in return for providing services of publicity and introduction rather than for acting on the client's behalf in any way.

The central concept of the law of agency is that of the agent's *authority*. If the agent acts without authority the principal is not bound by the transaction, either to the third party or to the agent himself (for instance, to pay commission). It is of the utmost importance, therefore, to determine the limits of the agent's authority in any particular case. Basically, the agent's authority rests upon the *consent* of the principal that the agent should act for him, and the first question is, 'What did the principal actually authorise the agent to do?' If the principal's instructions to the agent are ambiguous they will generally be given the interpretation most favourable to the agent and the third party, so that the principal may find that he has authorised more than he actually intended to authorise. Also, if instructions are given in general terms they will be held to authorise the agent to do all acts which are reasonably incidental to the acts authorised.

As a rule, the expression of the principal's consent will precede the transaction, but, except in one case, a subsequent consent is equally effective (so-called 'ratification'). Ratification is not possible where the principal is 'undisclosed'. It is not necessary for the agent to reveal the *identity* of his principal, but if the fact that the 'agent' purports to be acting on behalf of another is also concealed the principal is said to be undisclosed. Besides his inability to ratify a previously unauthorised transaction, the undisclosed principal is also exposed to certain risks which do not normally affect a disclosed principal—in particular he may be hard hit by the insolvency of the agent.

Although the principal's consent is the starting-point of the enquiry into the agent's authority, it is not the whole story. The legitimate interests of the third party sometimes require that the agent's acts be treated as authorised when, in fact, they are not. If an agent is employed in circumstances in which such an agent customarily has his principal's consent to do certain acts it is only right that third parties should not be prejudiced by any limitation on this customary authority in the particular instance, unless they actually know that the agent's authority is less than it customarily is. Thus a person instructing an auctioneer to sell his house will be bound by a memorandum of sale signed by the auctioneer on his behalf, even though it was signed in disregard of his express instructions, because it is usual for an auctioneer to have authority to do this. His limitation of the auctioneer's authority will not assist him, unless the purchaser knew of it.

A similar rule applies where the principal 'holds out' another as being his agent, that is, acts in such a way as to create the *appearance* of consent or stands by while the agent creates the appearance of consent. The principal is bound by acts which he has apparently authorised, even though he never in fact consented to the agent's performing them on his behalf, or had withdrawn a consent once given. Thus, a husband is not, as a general rule, liable to pay his wife's bills (the ordinary expenses of running the household excepted), but if he permits his wife to obtain credit in his name and pays the bills without question he is creating the impression that the wife will continue to have his authority to purchase goods in his name. If he changes his mind it is pointless for him just to inform his wife of this. His liability will continue until he has also informed the creditors who rely on his apparent willingness to pay his wife's bills. As in the previous case of the auctioneer, no third party can rely

84

on the appearance of authority if he knows that in reality there is none.

Where the agent acts with authority, either real or apparent, according to the principles just discussed, the transaction has the same effect as if it had been made by the principal in person. As a general rule (there are minor exceptions), the agent drops out of the picture altogether, and neither acquires rights nor incurs liabilities with regard to the third party. Where the agent acts without authority, the principal is not bound by the agent's acts, and the agent himself is liable to pay damages to the third party for any loss caused by his purporting to act when he had no authority to do so, and this quite apart from any question of fraud or dishonesty by the agent.

(C) COMPANIES AND PARTNERSHIPS

A. J. Boyle

TODAY MOST BUSINESSES larger than the small shop on the corner are organised in the form either of a partnership or of a limited company. A group of two or more individuals who wish to carry on a business with a view to profit may form a partnership between them without any of the formal procedure or publicity which the registration of a company entails. However, a partnership presupposes mutual confidence between the parties, sharing of profits and losses (not necessarily equal sharing) and an equal right of all partners to participate in the running of the business. In view of the unlikelihood of a successful venture with a large number of partners, the Companies Act (1948) requires that a business association of more than twenty members must be registered as a company and may not take the form of a partnership.[1] On the other hand, a business of less than twenty members can be formed as a company or converted from a partnership into a company. Indeed, even someone trading by himself may incorporate his business by converting it into a 'one-man' company. In fact, two people are necessary to form and run a 'one-man' company. But the second may be a nominee of the first and need take virtually no part in the Company's activities: the trader's wife is an obvious candidate for the job.

In English law a partnership is an association of people in which the 'partnership' has no separate legal existence. Whatever is done by or for the partnership is, in law, done by or for the partners. A company, on the other hand, has its own legal personality distinct from that of its members, the shareholders. A company holds its own property, makes its own contracts, and can sue and be sued for breach of contracts and for other wrongs. Thus, when you trade with a company your contracts are made with the company itself through the agency of the directors and other officers who act on its behalf. In the case of a partnership you do business directly with the partners through the agency of whichever partner deals with you. They all become personally liable on contracts made on their behalf.

Limited Liability

The major commercial advantage which is conferred by an incorporated business is that of limited liability. The overwhelming majority of companies, private as well as public, are registered as 'limited' companies. In simple terms this means that even if the company is forced into liquidation by its creditors on the ground of insolvency, the shareholders, so long as their shares are fully paid up, are not liable to meet the company's debts. They will, of course, lose what they have already invested in the company, but nothing more, since the liability of shareholders is limited to the extent of their share capital. If the company has 'uncalled' capital (that is, some or all of the shares are not fully paid) the shareholders must pay what is still outstanding on their shares. In a partnership, by contrast, each of the partners is jointly liable with all the other partners to the full extent of the partnership debts both during the existence of the partnership and when it is dissolved. Even if a company is registered without the usual advantage of limited liability, the obligation of shareholders differs from that of partners. Since an unlimited company still has legal personality, the shareholders cannot be sued for the company's debts during its life, but become fully liable to contribute to its losses if it is wound up insolvent. Such unlimited companies are only very occasionally formed for banking or insurance purposes. Here the unlimited liability of very wealthy shareholders, with large resources employed elsewhere, may be an important reserve asset for the company.

It is also possible, though again it is very unusual, for some but not all of the members of a partnership to enjoy limited liability. In the very small number of partnerships registered under the Limited Partnership Act (1907) a distinction is made between 'sleeping' partners and 'managing' partners, of whom there must be at least one. Sleeping partners may limit their liability to the amount of capital that they have contributed to the partnership. This privilege is subject to the condition that they take no active part in the management of the business, which they must leave to the managing partners. The managing partners, however, remain fully liable for their firm's losses as in an ordinary partnership. Very little use has been made of the limited partnership because the conversion of a partnership into a small private company will give limited liability to all the shareholders, even though they also manage the company as directors. However, members of certain professions (such as solicitors and accountants) are not allowed to incorporate. Here a limited partnership may be of use where a partner wishes to retire from practice while leaving his capital in the partnership and sharing in the profits. But where things go badly in such a partnership the sleeping partner may be tempted to intervene in the business, and if he does so he loses the protection of limited liability. In seeking to save his investment he may lose all he has.

The Other Advantages of Incorporation

In addition to limited liability a number of advantages
follow from the separate legal existence of a company which
the members of a partnership do not enjoy. The device of
incorporation insulates the shares which represent the
members' intangible interest in their company from the
property of the company itself. This is not so in the case of a
partnership. Thus the death, bankruptcy, insanity or retirement of a partner will require that his share of the partnership be realised. This will often lead to a dissolution of the
partnership as a whole, unless the other partners have been
given an option to purchase their former partner's interest
and are able and willing to do so. By contrast, a shareholder
can realise his interest by simply transferring his shares without affecting the company's property or its continued
existence. There will usually be restrictions, however, on the
right to transfer in the case of a private company. Thus the
directors may have a discretion as to whether or not to
register the transferee. Again, a company's assets are not
answerable in any way for the debts or bankruptcy of a
shareholder. Here it is the shares of a judgment debtor or a
bankrupt which will be affected. In a partnership the share
of the partnership property belonging to a bankrupt partner
will vest in his trustee in bankruptcy whether or not, as
between the solvent partners, the partnership is wound up.
Similarly, a creditor who obtains judgment for a separate
non-partnership debt against a partner may obtain an order
charging that partner's share of the property and profits of
the partnership and appointing a receiver to enforce the
charge.

Today perhaps the most crucial factor which determines
whether or not a small business should be incorporated is
that of taxation. Here the answer depends on the size of
the trading income of the business. At the lower levels there
may be no advantage or even a greater tax burden resulting
from incorporation. At higher levels of trading income, conversion into a private company brings increasing advantage.
The introduction of the new system of corporation tax has,

moreover, marginally increased the tax advantage of incorporating a small business.

The Protection of Creditors

The advantage that limited liability gives both to the large and to the small investor is the insulation of their other resources from the hazards to which their investment in risk capital is exposed. This protection was an essential requirement for the development of large-scale industrial and commercial enterprise. The objection that was so long urged against limited liability was that the protection of shareholders was necessarily bought at the expense of the company's creditors. Parliament, having conferred limited liability, attempted to protect creditors by requiring the public disclosure of information about the company's constitution and share capital. Information about its directors and shareholders, as well as its accounts, must be filed with the Registrar of Companies in the Company's annual returns. In addition, the company has to keep further registers open to inspection at its registered office and fly the word 'limited' at the masthead in all its dealings. This last was originally intended to warn potential creditors of the risks they ran, though it has long since ceased to have this effect. Another rule, which was evolved by the courts with the subsequent assistance of the legislature, prohibited the return of capital to the shareholders except in the event of a winding up after the company's other liabilities have been met. There are certain exceptions to this rule, such as a reduction of capital authorised by the court or the redemption of redeemable preference shares. These are provided for by statute subject to stringent safeguards.

Private Companies

The measures we have discussed might be thought to provide sufficient protection for creditors, but the development of the small private company owned in effect by a single shareholder, the 'one-man Company', has again put the unwary and unsecured creditor at a disadvantage. The decision of the House of Lords in *Saloman* v. *Saloman & Co. Ltd.* in 1897[2] finally established the rigid distinction between a shareholder and his company. Even though Saloman was the only shareholder, apart from a few nominees among the members of his family, the House of Lords refused to 'pierce the corporate veil'. Saloman had incorporated his then prosperous business by selling it to the company he had formed at an honest but highly optimistic price. This price was paid in the form of shares and £10,000 of debentures secured by floating charge over all the company's assets. When later, due to unforeseen events, the business failed and the company was wound up, the ordinary creditors could not be paid. The assets left were only sufficient to satisfy the debenture holder as a secured creditor, and nothing was left for the other creditors. The House of Lords, unlike the lower courts, would not accept the argument that the whole transaction was a sham, and therefore Saloman should lose the protection of limited liability and personally contribute to the company's losses. There was no evidence of fraud, as all the previous creditors had been paid at the time the company was formed, and Saloman had later mortgaged the debentures in a vain endeavour to save the company by raising more money.

This case illustrates perhaps not so much the dangers of limited liability for creditors as the obvious advantage of being a secured as opposed to an unsecured creditor. In the floating charge companies possess a very flexible but effective way of mortgaging their assets. In contrast to an ordinary mortgage of land or a bill of sale mortgaging goods, a floating charge 'floats' over the whole undertaking of the company, including its cash, stock in trade and future assets. It can be made to 'crystallise' by the appointment of a receiver whenever the debenture holders have reason to fear that their loan to the company is in danger of not being repaid. Subject to any prior charges over the company's property, the floating charge will crystallise over all the assets the company possesses at that time. Because of certain provisions in the law governing bankruptcy and bills of sale, this very useful form of security cannot be used by individual traders or partners. One of the principal attractions in forming a private company is that a floating charge duly registered by a company is a valid form of security. It allows the ordinary stock in trade and accounts receivable of a small business (often its main assets) to be dealt with in the course of business while at the same time being pledged as security to a bank or other institution which provides finance for the development of the company.

Since the *Saloman* decision Parliament has further encouraged the incorporation of businesses by individual traders and small partnerships by giving special privileges to private companies provided they satisfy certain conditions. Such companies must limit the number of shareholders to fifty; they must restrict the transfer of shares and they may not issue invitations to the public to invest in their shares. The procedure for forming such a company is much simplified and is consequently cheaper. A minimum of two shareholders will suffice. There need be only one director and a company secretary, who could be the same persons as the two shareholders. Even more substantial advantages are conferred on 'exempt private companies' so long as they continue to satisfy the Registrar that they are genuine family concerns and are not subsidiaries of larger companies or financed to any considerable extent by outside investors. These exempt companies need not file their accounts annually with the Registrar. They may make loans to directors and need not have their accounts professionally audited.

When such secrecy is coupled with limited liability the danger for the unwary creditor is obvious. This is more especially the case since English company law, while prohibiting the return of share capital once this has been subscribed, does not demand that a company should issue sufficient shares for cash to have a minimum working capital to start life with. In the case of public companies which issue prospectuses inviting the public to subscribe for their shares, there are safeguards imposed by the Companies Act and Stock Exchange regulations as to the information which must be given in the prospectus. Liability is imposed for false or misleading statements. The freedom to form under-capitalised private companies with limited liability can clearly lend itself to abuse. A bank or other experienced creditor, lending a large amount of money over a period of time, can obtain security for its loan in the form of a floating charge or a personal guarantee from the directors. They will also examine the company's books. However, the small creditor who may extend credit for goods or services supplied to such a company in a more informal fashion needs better protection.

The Jenkins Committee, in its report on company-law reform in 1962,[3] wisely recommended that the special privileges of exempt private companies should be abolished, but they did not propose that there should be any new rule about minimum capital. They maintained that no workable criteria could be laid down for all types of company. However, if the Registrar of Companies were given the power, when a company is formed, to determine the minimum capital according to a flexible statutory standard the practical difficulties need not be so great as the Committee seemed to think.

Suggested Reading

BORRIE & DIAMOND, *The Consumer, Society and the Law*, Penguin.
GOWER, *Modern Company Law*, Parts One and Two, Stevens.
SLATER, *Mercantile Law*, Pitman.

NOTES

[1] The New Companies Bill (1966) will, if enacted, abolish this restriction on the number of partners in the case of certain professional partnerships (solicitors, accountants and stockbrokers). Since these professions do not allow their members to incorporate, the present limit of twenty members to a partnership is unduly burdensome.

[2] (1897) A.C. 22.

[3] Cmnd. 1749 (1962). All the privileges of exempt private companies would be abolished if the new Companies Bill is passed into law in its present form.

7

Crime & Punishment

T. E. James

The General Nature of a Crime

LAWYERS THEMSELVES find it very difficult to define a crime with any precision. The fact that criminal proceedings are involved is generally accepted as sufficient for the practising lawyer; it is only the theorist who is troubled. It is apparent that the criminal law consists of acts and omissions which are proscribed either by statute or the common law which the judges have evolved. A rough classification of crimes may be made into three groups:

1. Personal offences, such as murder, rape and larceny.

2. Offences against the dignity and security of the State, such as conduct affecting public order, treason and blasphemy.

3. Offences relating to social welfare, such as selling adulterated food, spitting in public places, evasion of income tax, less-serious motoring offences and public health provisions.

The personal offences have been condemned for the most part since time immemorial in civilised as well as primitive societies. In early primitive communities these were not apparently considered as offences against society, but were punished by retaliation by the person or family. This evolution in relation to murder is well described in Appendix 7 of the Royal Commission Report on Capital Punishment 1949–53.[1] In early stages of development in a community the offences punished by the society or the group were those

93

against the security of the State, since they endangered the whole community. Gradually, it may be said, all offences against the individual (personal offences) came to be regarded as offences against the security of the State. Ultimately, in more sophisticated communities the tendency seems to be to regard all offences as involving considerations of social or public welfare.

The improvement in communications, economic pressures in highly competitive societies and improved education among other things have given rise to the need for a new definition of crime. For example, bigamy was first made a crime in the reign of James I; it was previously only an offence dealt with by the ecclesiastical courts. Incest became a criminal offence only in 1908. The White Slave traffic was controlled in 1885 by the Criminal Law Amendment Act after an intentionally created scandal under circumstances in which publicity could not be avoided. Today there is a growing body of minor statutory offences, dealt with in the Magistrates' Courts, as well as a series of statutes aimed at combating violence in public, such as the Air Guns and Shot Guns Act, 1962, controlling the wild behaviour of juveniles; the Restriction of Offensive Weapons Act, 1959, controlling the use of knives with automatic blades; the Prevention of Crimes Act, 1953, relating to the possession of offensive weapons in public places, and the Firearms Act, 1965, which controls the possession of firearms in certain circumstances.

It has been said that no society can survive unless its basic values, institutions and education are integrated with one another.[2] For the purpose of the integration of values, conduct norms or accepted standards are laid down by the criminal law, which enforces them, or by custom or convention backed by social disapproval. Alongside, social control is exercised through the rules of institutions such as the Church, the University and professional bodies. These institutions represent values which have been incorporated into the social framework and constitute important units in the structure of society. These rules are enforced in general not by legal sanctions but by convention or ostracism.

There are various other methods of classifying crimes, for instance for statistical purposes. Here a distinction has to be made between indictable and non-indictable offences. The former are the more serious crimes and involve trial by the High Court or Quarter Sessions with a jury. Some of the indictable offences today, under certain circumstances, are tried summarily in the Magistrates' Court in the same way as non-indictable offences. The classification of indictable offences for statistical purposes by the Home Office include offences against the person, sexual offences, crimes of violence and offences against property. The non-indictable offences are of a very mixed kind, but the motor offences included here comprise a huge number overshadowing all the other offences. It must always be remembered that by far the largest proportion of criminal cases are dealt with by the Magistrates' Courts. There is invariably a right of appeal, but nevertheless the more serious crimes, the indictable ones, and the appeals heard by the High Court, Quarter Sessions, the Divisional Court or the Court of Appeal (Criminal Division), form numerically only a small proportion of all the criminal offences brought to trial.

i. The Essentials of a Crime. A basic principle of the criminal law is that to establish legal guilt there must be a criminal act (*actus reus*) and a criminal intent (*mens rea*). The criminal trial is concerned with the proof that the accused did the act which is prohibited by law. The criminal intention is never in itself sufficient; thus for an attempt to steal there must be some act to evidence the intention. The intention to commit a crime is complicated by the fact that offences require different intentions; for example, it must be proved in a case of theft that the accused took and carried away something capable of being stolen without the consent of the owner, fraudulently and without a claim of right made in good faith. In a prosecution for murder 'malice aforethought' (a highly technical expression) on the part of the accused must be proved. The intents required therefore differ with the various offences as defined by the law. In general, however, it is essential for the criminal act and the necessary criminal intent to take place at the same time.

This statement of the basic principle is, of course, an over-simplification, for a person can commit a criminal offence by *omitting* to do an act. This can occur where the law places a special duty on a person which he fails to fulfil, for example, where a parent wilfully neglects a child in a manner likely to cause injury to its health. There is always in these cases a special relationship between the accused and the person offended against, such as occurs when a doctor or surgeon treats a patient.

Again, there are a very large number of minor offences which have been created by statutes and which require no criminal intent at all. The act is sufficient. These are called offences of strict liability and are dealt with in the Magistrates' Courts. A good example is the selling of adulterated food, where the vendor need not be shown to have any knowledge of the condition of the food. Another example is the driving of a motor vehicle without insurance. It might well be argued that, in a sophisticated society such as ours where a degree of education is given to all, it is justifiable to impose a liability for an act alone having regard to the harm that could be done to the public and the very great difficulty in such cases of proving an intent.

ii. The Defences. There are also a number of defences that an accused person can make use of and which may enable the accused to escape conviction, even though the criminal act and intent are proved. Thus, the accused may raise the defence of mistake, which would generally be evidence that there was no criminal intent. For instance, a man who was not a registered medical practitioner was charged with wilfully and falsely using the title of physician. He was charged with an offence under the Medical Act, 1958, but was acquitted on the ground that he genuinely believed he was entitled so to describe himself. It is to be observed that the accused had not been brought up in England. Force or duress and drunkenness may likewise be pleaded to negative the criminal intent, but these defences are strictly limited by the law.

Finally, a defence of considerable complexity is insanity. Insanity in the sense that the accused is suffering from some disability which renders him unfit to plead may, however, arise before or during trial. Such a finding would prevent the trial taking place or would discontinue it if once begun. Lawyers have a test of insanity as a defence which was laid down by the M'Naghten Rules in 1843. These Rules have been much criticised, particularly by the medical world, including the psychiatrists. The legal test for insanity is a rule-of-thumb, practical one which certainly does not cover all the cases which would come within the psychiatric categories of psychosis, such as, for example, schizophrenia, manic depression, G.P.I. (general paresis). Another objection by the medical profession is that legal insanity does not cover cases of uncontrollable impulse nor, perhaps, partial insanity. Insanity used as a rule to be pleaded only in prosecutions for murder, though it was available as a defence to any offence charged. The reason was that if found guilty of murder but insane the accused would not be executed but detained in Broadmoor during Her Majesty's Pleasure. If the offence was other than murder the accused would prefer the ordinary punishment rather than the indefinite period in Broadmoor. Today the verdict takes the form of an acquittal, which is much more logical, and the accused is found not guilty by reason of insanity. He is then treated as though he were subject to a hospital order, with a restriction on discharge for an unlimited period. Since capital punishment has been abolished, at least till 1970, it will be interesting to see whether much use is made of the defence of insanity which, if successful, would result in an indeterminate period in Broadmoor as opposed to a life sentence of imprisonment. In either case the Home Secretary could release the accused at his discretion. Insanity may nullify the criminal intent or the criminal act. In the latter case the mental state may be such that the accused does not know the physical nature of his act, for example, if he puts the baby on the fire instead of a log. Within the legal definition of insanity can be found cases of insane automatism, such as epilepsy, which result in killing during a trance. These cases are covered by the M'Naghten Rules. The act cannot, however, be criminal if it is involuntary and uncontrolled. This is called sane automatism and occurs when some disease, such as a coma resulting from diabetes, or some outside force, like a blow on the head, incapacitates the accused, who then commits an act which would otherwise be criminal. For instance, the accused while driving a car may have lost control of it through his condition, and as a result killed a person walking on the footpath.

Finally, in a case where murder is charged the defence of diminished responsibility is available. If successful this would result in a finding by the Court of manslaughter not murder, and the sentence could be any term up to life imprisonment. Diminished responsibility was introduced to cover some cases which would not be covered by the defence of insanity under the M'Naghten Rules, for example, cases of irresistible impulse. It relates only to murder charges and requires proof of an abnormality of mind which substantially impairs mental responsibility.

iii. Parties to a Crime. Persons who assist an accused to commit a criminal act which is punishable by a sentence of imprisonment for a term of five years (an arrestable offence), may themselves become subject to the criminal law. These persons may be present aiding the principal offender at the time of the offence or may advise or knowingly give assistance before the offence is committed. They would be liable to the same extent as the principal offender. In addition, anyone assisting a person who has committed an arrestable offence by hindering his prosecution or arrest may be guilty of an offence.

iv. Conclusion. Reference has already been made to the considerable discussion by eminent lawyers and sociologists as to whether the law and morality coincide. There is no doubt that the statutory offences have aimed at adopting measures against certain social dangers which have been generally reprehended. There are also some common-law offences which may be invoked 'to conserve not only the safety and order but also the moral welfare of the State'. Such was the opinion of Viscount Simonds in the case of *Shaw* v. *Director of Public Prosecutions* [1962][3] when the House of Lords asserted the right of the courts to continue to expand the scope of the criminal law. In this case it was decided by this high authority that it constituted an offence for one or more people to conspire to commit a public mischief by an agreement to corrupt public morals. This decision leaves a very wide discretion in the hands of the Court in relation to public morals. But as Lord Denning, Master of the Rolls, pointed out in his address to the Magistrates' Association in 1960: whatever might be said about the difference between sin and crime, it was to his mind quite clear that the whole of our criminal law must be backed by the strong moral force of a public opinion which condemned wrongdoing. This brings us back to the statement referred to earlier, namely, that no society can survive unless its basic values, institutions and education are integrated with one another.

Juveniles

Apart from the aim of punishment to deter persons from pursuing a life of crime which will be considered later, there is a whole section of our law which relates to juveniles. The Juvenile Courts, which were set up in 1908, are designed to deal with young offenders and also juveniles who are in need of care, protection or control. The Juvenile Court has, then, a criminal and a civil jurisdiction. The criminal function of the Juvenile Court explains itself: the juvenile is brought before the Court for an offence against the criminal law. Since today anyone under ten years of age cannot be charged, being presumed to be incapable of committing a crime, he will be dealt with, if necessary, under the other category. The care, protection or control jurisdiction comprises a wide variety of juveniles and is defined to include those not receiving the protection of a reasonably good parent and those who are falling into moral danger or bad associations. It also includes juveniles who are beyond parental control and those who fail to attend school.

In general, whether the proceedings in the Juvenile Court are civil or criminal, the juvenile has to be under seventeen years of age. This age limit is not rigid, for it does not matter, in certain specified cases, if he reaches seventeen in the course of the proceedings.

All juveniles are naturally prone to commit minor offences in the process of growing up. The less well to do, of course, have less opportunity of carrying out their malpractices to their satisfaction in the home or garden. The shame that is felt, at least in the case of the lower-income groups, when one of their children is brought before the Court, shows a healthy respect for the law; but unless the police exercise a wise discretion when bringing a juvenile before the Court, grave injustice might result from the point of view of social stigma, quite apart from the findings of the Court. It is obvious that those who come before the Juvenile Court are not a representative cross-section of the community as a whole.

Young people between seventeen and twenty-one are dealt with in the ordinary courts; but they receive the benefit of special treatment when the sentence of the Court is given. (See Appendix page 108.)

Owing to the fact that a high percentage of the juveniles appearing before a Juvenile Court plead guilty to offences charged and as a result of a movement that considers more preventive work could be done by less formal proceedings, the introduction of Family Councils and Family Courts has been envisaged. The Juvenile Courts would be abolished, and in their place cases over which they had jurisdiction would be brought before the Family Council, consisting of persons now working in the children's service and others with special understanding and experience of children. If the facts were disputed by the child or the parents the matter would be referred to the Family Court in order that these might be judicially determined. The Family Court would consist of a panel of justices chosen for their capacity to deal with young people. Only persons under sixteen years of age would be subject to this procedure. Young Offenders' Courts would be set up to deal with offences by those persons between sixteen and twenty-one, though certain of the more serious crimes (such as murder, rape, robbery) would be sent by these courts to higher courts for trial.

The general intention behind the suggested Family Courts is that the stigma of criminality should be avoided and that more flexibility should be allowed to the Court in treatment and supervision of the juvenile's subsequent progress. The new proposals, if they ultimately become law, would remove young people under sixteen so far as possible from the jurisdiction of the courts. The Family Councils would then deal with each undisputed case in consultation and agreement with the parents. In disputed cases reference would have to be made to the Family Courts so as to ensure that the interests of the child were protected by all the present legal safeguards. If the Family Court found the facts proved, then the child would come back to the Family Council for a decision as to his treatment, with the agreement and assistance of his parents if possible.

The effect of these new proposals would leave most of the present methods of treatment or punishment unchanged, except for the fine. Family Councils would not find it appropriate to require the voluntary payment of a fine with the parents' agreement. Compensation for loss as a result of a child's conduct could be allowed. Family Courts would be unaffected by this change.

Punishment

The lawyer's function in relation to the criminal law may be said to be threefold, namely, the interpretation of the law with particular regard to safeguarding the liberty of the subject; the control of the proceedings through rules of evidence and procedure, and the control of the sentence once there is a conviction. It is with the third function that we are here concerned. (See Appendix, page 108.)

Until quite recent times the treatment of criminals was almost entirely concerned with punishment. Strictly, treatment should include only methods involving direct personal approach to the offender, such as probation but not conditional and absolute discharge. However, treatment is often used in its wider sense, namely to include all methods prescribed by law for dealing with the criminal; in this sense punishment and treatment have a similar meaning. 'In deciding the approximate sentence, a Court should always be guided by certain considerations. The first and foremost is the public interest. The criminal law is publicly enforced, not only with the object of punishing crime, but also in the hope of preventing it.'[4] Thus, the sentence of the court may deter the particular offender from future criminal conduct —this is called special deterrence or special prevention; or it may deter others who might be tempted to try crime as seeming to offer easy money—this is called general deterrence or general prevention. For this reason our law does not fix the sentence for a particular crime, but fixes a maximum sentence and leaves it to the Court to decide what is, within the maximum, the appropriate sentence for each criminal in the particular circumstances of each case. The Court may be lenient or severe having regard to each crime and also to each criminal.

i. Theories of Punishment. Lawyers commonly discuss punishment with a view to what it should achieve according to its conscious purpose. Usually, the theories of punishment are then put under four headings:

- (*a*) The Retributive Theory.
- (*b*) The Preventive Theory.
- (*c*) The Deterrent Theory.
- (*d*) The Reformative Theory.

(*a*). The retributive theory or expiation. This is the old notion of an eye for an eye, that is, a thief should have his hand cut off, a perjuror should lose his tongue. It is sometimes referred to as the *lex talionis* and is based on revenge. Even today, when a particularly horrible crime is committed, a feeling is stirred up among the general public that demands retribution. Though this is clearly a profoundly rooted reaction, based probably on fear, the modern trend is to disallow this rather crude and deep feeling when considering the sentence of the court. A very important element has been introduced today in this connection, and that is the need for the criminal to make restitution or compensation to the victim. The law does provide that restitution or compensation orders may be made in certain circumstances. The most far-reaching of these relates to compensation which can be ordered only when the court makes a probation order or absolutely or conditionally discharges the offender. Under this particular provision, if the criminal is sent to prison, then no compensation can be ordered.

A very interesting development has been the setting up of a Board which can award compensation out of public funds to the victims of crimes of violence. The Government refused to accept the principle that the State is liable for injuries caused to people by the criminal acts of others; but recognised the existence of a public sense of responsibility for the innocent victim. Compensation is paid therefore in certain cases, but it is an *ex gratia* payment, that is, no legal obligation is accepted. The scheme came into force on August 1st, 1964, and is operating reasonably successfully. Anyone who suffers personal injury as a direct consequence of a criminal offence, or by trying to arrest an offender or to prevent a crime, can apply. If the injuries are fatal the victim's dependants may apply. Certain claims will not be entertained, for example, a claim arising from injuries caused by a motor car unless the car was deliberately used to run down the victim. Similarly, claims by a member of the offender's family living with him at the time, for example arising from an attack by a father on his daughter, will not be allowed. The amount of compensation that may be awarded is assessed on the same principles as those adopted by the courts, but with certain limitation.

Much thought has been given in recent times to the introduction of methods whereby the criminal himself would be enabled to compensate in cash or public work for his crime, whether it be one of violence or against property. This is perhaps viewed as a means of rehabilitating and reforming the offender rather than retribution, and will be mentioned in that connection.

(b). The preventive theory or, as it is sometimes called, special deterrence is aimed at deterring the criminal himself from further depredation on the public. In the old days capital punishment or transportation to Virginia or Australia was an effective example of this theory. Capital punishment, at least for the time being, and transportation have been abolished; but the courts can impose a long sentence of imprisonment. Today it is generally agreed that the most effective way of preventing a repetition of an offence is to reform the offender, if this is possible.

(c). The deterrent theory, sometimes referred to as general deterrence or prevention, is directed to the deterring of others from committing a similar offence by the severity of the punishment imposed. It is really impossible to prove that this kind of sentence has an effect, though it is generally assumed to do so. The Notting Hill race riots, when a number of youths, of otherwise excellent character, attacked coloured members of the community without any provocation, is usually cited as an example. Severe sentences of imprisonment were imposed, and there is no doubt that such wanton conduct did seem to be controlled as a result. The need for capital punishment to prevent persons committing murder is often argued on the basis of general deterrence. Lord Gardiner, the present Lord Chancellor, has argued in relation to capital punishment that, if it is to be asserted that the death sentence deters would-be murderers, the persons alleging this to be so must prove its correctness before the theory is accepted.[5] Of course, by its very nature the proposition, that a punishment deters others from committing a similar crime, is unprovable with any degree of accuracy or reliability. Judges often do say, however, when on circuit, that they are imposing a certain punishment because there is too much crime of that particular kind in the area. The public as a whole tends to accept that such sentences are effective as deterrents.

(d). The reformative theory is very much emphasised today. Clearly this is the most satisfactory approach, whether considered from the humane or purely practical aspect. A distinction must here be made between adult offenders and those under twenty-one (see below). Certainly all punishment should be primarily directed to rehabilitation and reformation; but, it is argued, rehabilitation may be achieved in some cases by straight punishment, such as corporal punishment.

ii. The Adult Offender. Today the trend is against punishment as such, and even sentences of imprisonment for adults are often considered to involve some form of treatment, with the exception of a few long-term sentences designed to keep the offender shut up and away from the public. The fine (see Appendix, page 108) might, however, be regarded as purely punitive, for it is paid to the State and is not used for compensation of the victim. It has been suggested that at least for persons sentenced to imprisonment, their pay should be sufficient for something to be set aside by way of restitution or compensation. Of course, it would be idle to pay prisoners a sufficient wage for this purpose unless in fact they earned it in prison. The problem of employment of prisoners is receiving considerable attention today. It must be remembered that there is a very high turnover of persons in any one prison, and a number of them are not capable of consistent work. Work could be done in prison for outside employers or on some of the many domestic tasks; work could be done outside prison, as happens to some extent today with agricultural work and maintaining sea defences; outside work could also be undertaken from hostels. Apart from all this, vocational training could be undertaken on a more extensive scale than is done at present. These are some of the ideas put forward by reformers; but there are very real difficulties in the path of such progress which must be overcome. In any case, before any progress can really be made a better system of classification of prisoners is required. It must not be overlooked that many persons sent to prison are mentally disturbed in some degree, for instance their delinquency may be basically neurotic, psycho-pathological or constitutional. For a number of these offenders treatment by drugs or psycho-therapy is more appropriate for re-habilitation than vocational training or application to pro-ductive work.

A list of the methods available to the Court on sentencing is set out in the Appendix to this chapter, together with a short explanation of each form of sentence, whether it be for an adult or a person under twenty-one. Over and above these methods available on sentencing, the Court may make a hospital or guardianship order, if the accused is suffering from some mental disability within the Mental Health Act, 1959. Such orders would result in treatment in a mental in-stitution, and an order restricting the patient's release for a period of time may be included.

Probation is, of course, a great stand-by, but is rarely appropriate for the more serious offences. Probation is essentially co-operative work between the offender and the probation officer in the open. Much depends here on the capacity of the offender to benefit from his association with the probation officer. There are types of offenders, such as the psycho-path and the so-called inadequate (who commits trifling and inexplicable offences), who cannot establish a personal relationship or do so only with the greatest diffi-culty.

iii. The Offender under Twenty-one. Persons under twenty-one are as a rule much more susceptible to influence and more malleable than the older delinquents. Much work is done by local authorities with statutory powers to take care of deprived children under seventeen and to assist in kind, or exceptionally in cash, children under eighteen with a view to promoting their welfare. These provisions are pre-ventive and designed to diminish the need for such children to be brought before the Juvenile Court. The civil and criminal jurisdiction of the Juvenile Court has already been referred to, as also has the suggested introduction of Family Councils and Family Courts to take their place. As the law stands today any person over ten, and under seventeen, who commits a criminal offence may be subjected to an order designed primarily to rehabilitate or reform him. From seventeen to twenty-one special considerations apply to sentencing, for example, a prison sentence should not be passed, but use should be made of borstal or a detention centre.

It is clear that young persons who have committed offences are much better material for treatment and for the application of the reformation theory. Moreover, if they can be set on the right lines the greater part of their lives is before them, and they will be able to contribute much more to the community.

Therefore, the severity of the law in regard to punishment or treatment is relaxed in the case of juveniles. No sentence of imprisonment may be imposed on anyone under seventeen, nor on a person between seventeen and twenty-one, except in unusual circumstances. Further, special treatment is afforded for offenders of varying ages under twenty-one; this may consist of a detention centre or remand home order, a fine, probation, committal to an approved school, or borstal, or resort to an attendance centre (see Appendix, page 108). Of course, neither the fine nor probation are peculiar to juveniles, but they are applied rather differently in such circumstances. For instance, the fine is conditioned usually by the juvenile's pocket money, and probation is carried out by specially experienced officers. A young offender may also be absolutely or conditionally discharged; but this form of order is equally applicable to adults, and there are no variations when used for juveniles.

iv. Conclusion. In order to get a proper perspective it is necessary to recollect that other severe methods of punishment were used throughout the world as well as in the United Kingdom during the last century or two. Transportation continued throughout the early half of the last century; corporal punishment only finally disappeared as a punishment imposed by the Court in 1948; capital punishment has only recently been abolished for a provisional five years, that is until 1970. Criticism is frequently heard of the punishments used today by the courts and, justifiable though these criticisms may be in an abstract humanitarian sense, it is important to realise what huge improvements have been made. This does not mean that we may be apathetic and self-satisfied, for there is still a very long way to go. A real breakthrough will, however, be made only if we have a better understanding of the types of persons who commit offences, their motive and background and a better knowledge of the appropriate methods of treatment or even punishment. Much careful, scientific work is being carried out on these particular problems, and there is no doubt that the lawyers will welcome any assistance in developing and improving the sentencing policy of the courts.

APPENDIX

The Present Methods of Treatment and Punishment of Offenders

The following is an explanatory note on the various methods open to the Court when sentencing an offender. The first four apply to offenders of all ages, and special observations have been made, where appropriate, as regards young persons. The remainder relate entirely to persons under twenty-one.

1. Imprisonment

This may roughly be regarded as either short term (eighteen months or under), medium length (eighteen months to three years) or long term (over three years). Prisons may be open, closed or medium secure, and provide for all the various lengths of sentences, except that local prisons, which receive short-term prisoners and committals from Court, are generally closed. In addition, where an offender has come repeatedly before the Court, has already served institutional treatment and is over twenty-one, he may be sentenced to corrective training for a period of two to four years; if he is over thirty and certain other considerations are satisfied he may be sentenced to preventive detention for a period of five (usually seven or eight is the minimum) to fourteen years. It has been recommended that preventive detention should be abolished and that the courts should be given power to impose an ordinary sentence of imprisonment up to ten years in certain more serious cases. Long-term imprisonment can have the most deadening effect on a prisoner, so that he becomes unsuited to live naturally in the world on release except with considerable difficulty. The aim is to sentence only those who are a danger to the community to long-term imprisonment, apart from offenders whom the Court considers require exemplary sentences, for example the famous Aylesbury train robbers.

Short sentences (six months or under) are generally regarded as unsatisfactory, since they disrupt the life of the offender's family and allow insufficient time for any training in the prison. Indeed, Magistrates' Courts are directed by statute not to pass a prison sentence on a first offender, unless there is no other method of dealing with him. Magistrates' Courts have a limited power of sentencing to prison (up to six months) depending on the offence.

Young Offenders. Imprisonment of those between seventeen and twenty-one is permitted only in special circumstances. A prison for young offenders is set apart for such cases. Sentences of imprisonment may not be passed on those under seventeen; borstals, attendance centres, approved schools and detention centres are used instead. In exceptional circumstances a wing of a prison is used for juveniles on remand.

2. *Probation*

This may be ordered for a period not exceeding three years when a person has been convicted of an offence. The Court has a very wide discretion as to the conditions which may be attached to a probation order, including a condition of mental treatment, for example a condition of residence in a particular area. Probation orders may be discharged or reviewed within certain limits, but failure to comply with the requirements of the order results in certain penalties or even a sentence as though the offender had only just been convicted of the offence. The offender must express his willingness to comply with the requirements of a probation order if he is over fourteen.

The condition in a probation order may be that of residence in an Approved Probation Home or Hostel. Such Homes are usually provided for juveniles, but may be for mothers who have neglected their children.

Fines may not be imposed in addition to probation, since this would militate against the co-operation which is essential between the probationer and the probation officer. However, compensation may be ordered as well as probation.

Young Offenders. In the Juvenile Courts specially experienced probation officers are available. If the juvenile is under fourteen there is no need for his consent to the requirements of a probation order.

The probation service is hard pressed today with a heavy burden of work, to which is being added the after-care of discharged or licensed offenders.

3. The Fine

This is particularly appropriate where the State need have no concern for the offender, for example, for a breach of police regulations (street disorders, or obstructing the traffic) or minor motoring offences. It is not reformative; but as a deterrent or preventive measure it needs to be adjustable to the accused's means. This is not always possible, since statutes generally set a limit to the maximum fine permitted for a specific offence. The advantage of the fine is that it does not interfere with the whole life of the offender; that is, he pays and returns to his daily routine. This may result therefore in the virtual disappearance of the penal aspect of the fine.

Statute has provided that time may be allowed for payment of a fine, and an enquiry may be undertaken as to means.

Young Offenders. The maximum fine for a child (under

fourteen) is ten pounds; the maximum for a young person (between fourteen and seventeen) is fifty pounds.

4. *Conditional and Absolute Discharge*

Where a person has been convicted of an offence the Court may discharge him absolutely or conditionally. The condition in the latter case being that he commits no offence during a specified period not exceeding twelve months from the date of the order. If there is a breach of the conditional discharge the offender may be dealt with as if he had just been convicted of the offence for which it was made.

It might be better to call an absolute discharge an unconditional one so as to avoid the impression that the offender had been acquitted.

These two orders may be made when, having regard to the circumstances, including the nature of the offence and the character of the offender, it is considered inexpedient to inflict punishment and a probation order is inappropriate.

Compensation may be ordered in addition to a conditional or absolute discharge.

5. *Borstals*

These are available for juveniles between fifteen and twenty-one years of age who have committed an offence punishable by imprisonment. The Court has, however, to be satisfied that it is expedient that the offender be detained for training for not less than six months and, if he is under seventeen, that there is no other appropriate method of dealing with him. The period of detention may not exceed two years, and the offender may be released after six months. On release he is under supervision until the expiration of two years. While under supervision he must comply with any requirements that may be specified; however, he may be released from supervision altogether, or alternatively, be recalled to borstal.

Today there is a certain flexibility provided whereby certain persons may be removed from prison to borstal or a detention centre when it is considered expedient. Furthermore, a juvenile in an approved school may be transferred to borstal if a Magistrates' Court so orders and other conditions apply.

6. Detention Centres

These are available for persons between fourteen and twenty-one. They are of two kinds, senior (over seventeen) and junior. For the most part they are used for males, though one for females does exist. Detention centres were introduced in 1948, and an order may be made in circumstances where an offence has been committed which could be punished by imprisonment apart from the restriction on age. These centres were originally envisaged as an alternative to corporal punishment.

The period of detention is short, usually the minimum period of three months, but in more serious cases or when the offender has attained seventeen it may be up to six months. There is compulsory after-care for a period of twelve months from release.

Studies have indicated that this form of detention is most successful where there is an absence of a number of previous convictions and of previous institutional experience and—in the case of junior centres—when there is an unsatisfactory home background.

7. Attendance Centres

These were introduced in 1948 and are now available for juveniles between ten and twenty-one years of age. This order may be made where a prison sentence could have been passed were it not for the offender's age. Junior centres (for those under seventeen) are as a rule run by the local police; senior centres, of which there are now two, are run by the local prison staff in one case, and by the police in the other.

The effect of this order is that the offender must attend at a centre generally for not more than twelve hours in aggregate, and in any case not more than twenty-four hours. The offender must not previously have been in prison, borstal, a detention centre or an approved school.

This method of treatment is of particular value when applied to a juvenile who is reasonably stable and has had little contact with the law hitherto. Its chief punitive effect is its nuisance value, that is, having to attend on Saturday afternoons.

8. Approved Schools

These are available for juveniles under seventeen who have committed an offence, punishable with imprisonment in the case of an adult. These schools are of three categories for boys (junior, intermediate, that is, for those thirteen to fifteen, and senior) and two for girls (junior, under fifteen, and senior). A child under ten should not be sent to an approved school unless he cannot otherwise be dealt with suitably.

These schools may be voluntary and of a particular religious persuasion or provided by the local authority. Classifying Approved Schools (and a Classifying Remand Home) have been set up throughout the country for purposes of allocating the juvenile to the school which is considered most appropriate.

The approved school order continues in general for a period of three years, but not so as to last beyond the age of nineteen. A person subject to this order may be released under supervision after six months, when he will be under compulsory after-care. This after-care continues for two years from the date of release or until he attains twenty-one, whichever is the earlier.

In furtherance of flexibility of institutional training a person under eighteen in prison or borstal may be transferred to an approved school. Also a juvenile over fifteen may be removed by the Magistrates' Court, under special circumstances, from an approved school to a borstal.

The particular value of an approved school order would be in the removal from a background that has given rise to delinquency. The complaint is often made by workers in approved schools that they get the juveniles too late.

9. Committal to a Remand Home

This is an order that may be made when, but for the age of the offender, a sentence of imprisonment could have been passed. The committal period is limited, and in any case may not exceed one month. It is available for girls or boys under seventeen, but a detention centre order must be made instead, for those between fourteen and seventeen, if such a centre is available.

A remand home may be used for the temporary removal of juveniles in approved schools who are seriously unruly or subversive.

Suggested Reading

W. A. ELKIN, *The English Penal System*, Pelican.
C. F. SHOOLBRED, *The Administration of Criminal Justice*, Pergamon Press.

NOTES

[1] Cmnd. 8932.
[2] Karl Mannheim, *Diagnosis of our Time*, Kegan Paul, 1943.
[3] A.C. 220 at p. 267.
[4] *R.* v. *Ball* (1951) 35 Cr. App. Rep. 164 *per* Hilbery, J. at p. 166.
[5] Gardiner, *Capital Punishment as a Deterrent*, Gollancz, 1956.

8

Law and the Family[1]

Naomi E. Michaels

THE FAMILY must have a claim to being the oldest of social institutions. Man's notions of the typical family unit have certainly evolved over the ages, and even at any one period of time the considerable ethnic, religious and cultural differences to be found in society ensure that the family does not mean precisely the same thing the world over. Nevertheless, the essential features of family life remain the same. The family consists of a small closely interwoven group of persons living communally, dividing their functions among themselves and sharing the use of property in common—all for the individual and collective benefit. By and large, the family regulates its own existence. Over the course of every family's evolution each individual member acquires rights and corresponding obligations towards the other members. Sometimes rights are more heavily stressed than obligations, as with young children, but this usually evens itself out in the course of time, perhaps by a change of family grouping. Not all family obligations are ones which are recognised by law in the sense that the law imposes sanctions against their non-performance. There is here a divergence between what many people would regard as their moral duty towards their near relatives and their legal duty in this respect. Thus, while society may censure a man for failing to provide for an elderly impoverished parent, no legal sanction is imposed. Yet, at the same time the State relies heavily upon individual fulfilment of family obligations both legal and moral, for any default in this regard will mean that the State will have to step in and assume responsibility. Of course, by no means every individual case of need is a result of another's wilful default in carrying out his or her obligations. It is inevitable that misfortunes of one kind or another will cause family breakdowns, but, whatever the reasons for the default, the result is the same. The State must take over where others have failed.

Although, as we have seen, society relies upon man's sense of moral as well as legal responsibility in the family sphere, precisely because there is this difference in the nature of his obligations, the family unit according to English law is comprised only of those individuals who are regarded as being under a legal responsibility towards each other. The relationships which incur such responsibility are those of husband and wife and parent and infant child.[2] Although, therefore, there may be others who share equally in the life of the family, they are not part of the family unit in its legal sense. The typical family unit according to law thus begins with a marriage, creating thereby the relationship of husband and wife, and continues with the procreation of children, creating thereby the relationship of parent and child. The survival of the family does not depend upon the continued co-existence of both these relationships, for either one may cease without causing total disintegration. A marriage may be brought to an end by death or divorce, but if there are infant children surviving the family continues. Likewise, unlike in the animal world, the obligations created by the institution of marriage do not cease simply because all offspring have attained their legal majority or passed out of the family unit. So, once created, a family does not cease to exist until both its constituent relationships have come to an end.

The Role of Family Law

The average family in this country is very little concerned with family law. The law certainly regulates its formation in that marriage is a legal institution and legal requirements must be observed to ensure validity. However, dissolution of the family will normally take place according to the natural course of events, that is by death in due course in the case of the husband–wife relationship and by attainment of majority, or marriage under that age, in the case of that of parent and child. The law does not seek to interfere with the day-to-day running of the household, for basically it is for the members to settle among themselves what their respective functions are to be, and they are not assisted by the law to resolve family disputes. Thus, in general, once a family has been created according to law, the law has no further part to play in its future. The law is there to deal with the abnormal family, and in this respect its function is basically twofold. It exists to regulate dissolution of the central marriage relationship where the parties have failed to keep it in being, and secondly, to ensure that breakdown of the husband–wife relationship, whether by normal or abnormal means, does not leave any of the individual members of the family unprovided for. This will be done by enforcing continued performance of family obligations, but, if necessary, by state intervention.

The Nature of Marriage in English Law

It will have been seen from the foregoing that the central feature of the family concept is marriage. It follows that a large part of family law is concerned with the law relating to the formation, annulment and dissolution of marriage. But, before one can embark on any discussion of these topics it is necessary to give some thought to what we understand by marriage as an institution. This is not to signify that marriage in English law bears some special esoteric meaning which differs from the popular conception, but only that, like the family concept itself, marriage has not meant the same thing at all times to all persons. For example, Roman Law in classical times had another institution closely resembling marriage, but better described as lying midway between marriage and concubinage. Nevertheless, the similarities between this institution and marriage necessitated a careful drawing of distinguishing factors. Today polygamy still flourishes in many parts of the world, and the flow of peoples to and from those parts has presented our courts with new problems in the field of family law. For it has not proved easy to apply the marriage laws of this country to polygamously married couples.

'Marriage, as understood in Christendom, may . . . be defined as the voluntary union for life of one man and one woman to the exclusion of all others.'[3] This definition of the English concept of marriage was given by the celebrated judge, Lord Penzance, in 1866. It serves equally well as our definition today, for it stresses the three essential features of marriage in this country. First, the union must be voluntary, for there can be no marriage without the free consent of both parties. Consent produced by force or fear is no true consent for this purpose. Likewise, consent may not be real if it is negatived by the existence of severe mental illness or a mistaken belief that the ceremony was something other than a ceremony of marriage. Cases of no consent are rare indeed today and must be very strictly proved, but the occasional example still occurs. Secondly, the union of marriage is said to be for life, but this does not signify that it is incapable of dissolution by a court of law, and nor did it so signify in 1866. Rather was Lord Penzance drawing attention to the fact that the union must be at least potentially for life in the sense that it cannot be brought to an end by the occurrence of a predetermined event, such as continuation in a state of childlessness for a period of ten years, or the attainment of legal majority by all the children of the marriage. Marriages in this country can be terminated only by death or by a decree of a court of law, and any attempt by the parties to dissolve their marriage without recourse to law is of no effect legally. Finally, the union must be monogamous. This is the only form of marriage which can be contracted in this country, even if the parties come from a country which permits polygamy, and conversely, persons of English origin, who although living elsewhere nevertheless retain their English affiliations, are incapable of entering into anything other than a monogamous marriage. Provided, however, that these three essential features are present, it is not in the least necessary that the parties to the marriage be Christians. In other words, all that *is* necessary is that they should have entered into a union which corresponds in its essentials to the English notions of marriage.

Creation of a Valid Marriage

i. Form. There are a number of formalities with which persons intending to marry have to comply. On the whole, however, they present no very great obstacle, and cheap and speedy marriage is still possible in this country. The practice of contracting 'clandestine' marriages in disregard of legal formalities was at one time effective to create valid binding unions, but this was put to an end in 1753. In that year Lord Hardwicke's Act made the publication of banns or the obtaining of a common licence essential prerequisites to marriage validity. Among other formalities rendered essential by that Act were the requirements that there be at least two witnesses present at the ceremony and that proper registers be kept. Civil marriage, without reference to ecclesiastical forms, was first introduced into the law in 1836, and our present law[4] permits a variety of forms. It is possible to contract a marriage according to the rites of the Church of England, a purely civil marriage in a register office or a marriage in a place of religious worship of the parties' choice by a combination of religious and civil forms. Lack of compliance with the forms prescribed by law is still not regarded as a serious impediment to marriage validity, and few marriages are set aside for want of formality. It is never possible for a marriage to be invalid because the parties have unwittingly failed to comply with formal requirements, for both must be guilty of knowing and wilful default before such a defect will render the marriage void.

ii. Capacity. Much more important than form in the contracting of a valid marriage is that there should be no legal impediment barring the parties, or one of them, either from marrying at all or from marrying each other. In English law a person cannot marry at all if he or she is already validly married to another or if he or she is under the age of sixteen. The parties cannot marry each other if they are related within the prohibited degrees of consanguinity or affinity. Between the ages of sixteen and twenty-one it is necessary to obtain parental consent in order to be free to marry, but any marriage contracted despite non-compliance with this requirement remains none the less valid (although certain criminal penalties may become applicable). The prohibited degrees of relationship do not today present a serious impediment. In medieval times prohibitions of inter-marriage by reason of near relationship were so extensive that if the law had been strictly observed it would have been almost impossible, at least in small communities, for persons to marry at all. However, even in those days dispensations could be obtained. Nowadays affinity, that is relationship created by a previous marriage, raises an impediment only in the ascendant–descendant line, so that while it is still impossible for a man to marry his former daughter-in-law, he can marry in the collateral line, for example, the former wife of his nephew. Blood-relationship, known as con-sanguinity, bars marriage in the ascendant–descendant line and also marriage between certain near collateral relatives, i.e. brother and sister, uncle and niece or aunt and nephew. First cousins may, however, intermarry.

It does not follow that persons who are under no legal impediment towards marriage and who have complied with the formalities prescribed by law are necessarily validly married. For quite apart from the possibility, already dis-cussed, that one or other of them may not have consented to the union, there is in English law a 'half-way house' be-tween void and valid marriages. This is the concept of the voidable marriage. Broadly speaking, the difference between a void and voidable marriage is that marriages are void when the parties have contravened a requirement of public policy so that it is in the public interest that they be pre-vented from regarding themselves as married. This means that the 'marriage' can be set aside not only by the parties themselves but also by anyone else who may have an interest in their affairs. On the other hand, where the defect is of a personal nature and society has no interest in the matter, it is entirely within the parties' own free choice whether to treat the marriage as continuing or to apply to a court for a decree of nullity of marriage. Such a marriage is said to be voidable, that is, valid unless and until one of the parties to it takes steps to have it annulled by a court of law. Moreover, the decision whether or not to accept or repudiate the marriage must be made with a reasonable degree of promptitude, for, in all fairness to the other spouse, a person cannot be allowed to raise a grievance of this type long after it has ceased to be of fundamental importance in the parties' personal relationships with each other. A marriage is voidable if one of the parties is physically incapable of consummating it sexually or wilfully refuses to consummate it. It is likewise voidable if one party, without knowledge of the matter complained of, contracts a marriage with a person who is either suffering from certain forms of mental illness, or has venereal disease in a communicable form, or is pregnant by some other person. However, in these three latter cases a petition to set aside the marriage must be presented to the court within a year of the ceremony, or the remedy will be lost. In the case of non-consummation of the marriage the time limit is not so strict, but delay in pursuing the remedy of nullity may well be an indication that the petitioner had ceased to regard the sexual union as of fundamental importance in his or her particular marriage relationship, so that it would be unjust to the other party to grant a decree of nullity at that stage.

Matrimonial Relief

A decree of nullity of marriage, whether on the ground that the marriage is void or voidable, is one of the matrimonial remedies of English law. With one exception, all nullity decrees are granted by reason of some defect existing at the time of the ceremony.[5] The other matrimonial remedies exist for an entirely different purpose. Their function is to provide relief from a union which has become intolerable to one of the parties by reason of the other's behaviour, and for that reason has broken down. These remedies are three in number: namely, divorce, judicial separation and restitution of conjugal rights, and they all lie only where the party seeking relief, called the petitioner, proves that the other party, called the respondent, has committed a matrimonial 'offence'. This means that the respondent must have been guilty of a breach of his or her matrimonial obligations which is sufficiently serious to give the petitioner just cause for regarding the marriage as at an end. Suits for matrimonial relief are antagonistic suits in the sense that the petitioner has to prove his grounds for relief and the respondent may or may not deny the existence of those grounds. The respondent may also seek to cross-charge the petitioner with matrimonial misconduct, so that the final result of the case may be that a decree is awarded to the respondent. If both parties prove their cases and the Court finds that morally speaking there is little to choose between them it may even grant decrees to both. The majority of petitions for matrimonial relief are, however, undefended, for frequently respondents have little interest in contesting them. Nevertheless, the framework of the antagonistic law-suit remains, since the respondent must be served with notice of the proceedings, and even if he elects to offer no answer to the petition, he is still the legal defendant in those proceedings. Moreover, even where no defence is offered, the Court by no means acts purely as a 'rubber stamp' to the petitioner's suit, for it has a duty to conduct enquiries into the truth of the facts alleged and may order its officers to submit a report.[6] As yet, therefore, it is not possible for matrimonial relief to be obtained simply upon the basis that both parties want it or that the marriage has utterly broken down. Neither of these factors is in itself sufficient, for there must also be grounds for relief in the form of a legally recognised type of misconduct. Unless the petitioner can prove that his grievances fulfil the requirements of the appropriate legal ground of relief, no remedy can be obtained.

By far the most important matrimonial remedy of English law is that of divorce. Leaving aside the decree of nullity of marriage, which in strict theory declares the parties never to have been validly married to each other, divorce is the only remedy which enables the parties to a valid marriage to remarry during each other's lifetime. There are four grounds of divorce available to either sex, namely, adultery, desertion for at least three years, cruelty and incurable insanity. A wife has in addition a right to petition for divorce on the ground of her husband's commission of certain unnatural offences. Of the grounds common to both sexes, insanity is clearly an exception to the general principle that normally relief will be granted only upon proof of the respondent's matrimonial misconduct. Divorce for insanity is, however, hedged about with many safeguards, and the Court has a duty to protect the interests of the afflicted spouse no less than those of the petitioner. In proportion to the other grounds of relief, few marriages are dissolved under this head. Occasionally also, the Court may find the matrimonial 'offence' of cruelty proved despite the fact that the respondent cannot be held morally responsible for his conduct by reason of some abnormal state of mind, but in general, adultery, desertion and the vast majority of cruelty cases all involve some degree of blameworthiness on the part of the respondent. The petitioner's conduct, too, is by no means irrelevant, in that he may be found to have waived his right to petition on the ground of the respondent's misconduct by agreeing to overlook it or, in the case of adultery, he may have actively encouraged it. In neither case will the petitioner be able to obtain a decree. Moreover, any reprehensible conduct on the petitioner's part, whether or not it conduced to the respondent's guilt, may mean that the Court is entitled to refuse to grant a decree because the petitioner is too unworthy to receive relief. Finally, the parties, if they have children under sixteen, must not be allowed to forget that they are parents even when they are raising grievances which on the face of them have nothing to do with the children. For no court may grant matrimonial relief (other than a decree of restitution of conjugal rights) unless it is satisfied that proper arrangements have been made for the care and upbringing of every child of the family under sixteen.

The other matrimonial remedies of English law may be dismissed fairly briefly, for they are of little importance in practice. A decree of judicial separation is no easier to obtain than a decree of divorce, for the grounds upon which both are available are almost identical, and the Court may refuse relief to the petitioner for the same reasons as in the case of divorce petitions. Judicial separation is a form of relief which may be preferable to those who have religious or other objections to divorce, for the effect of the decree is to preserve the formal marriage bond while releasing the parties from their mutual obligation to live together and at the same time regulating the terms upon which they are to live apart and carry out their obligations towards their children. While both are still alive, however, neither is free to remarry, and for this reason the remedy sometimes becomes a weapon in the hands of a spouse who wishes to be vindictive. There is nothing in the law to compel an aggrieved spouse to seek any form of matrimonial relief at all, and there is certainly no provision which seeks to compel him to petition for divorce rather than judicial separation. Unhappily, therefore, a spouse who has no interest in retaining the marriage bond as such, but yet is not interested in remarriage, sometimes elects to 'spite' the other by denying him or her the chance of remarriage also. Nevertheless, because there are persons who may have genuine reasons for preferring judicial separation to divorce, the remedy has been retained.

Restitution of conjugal rights, the remaining matrimonial remedy yet to be discussed, is of even less practical significance. As its name implies, the decree declares that the petitioner is entitled to have the matrimonial cohabitation restored and orders a deserting spouse to return to the matrimonial home. However, there are no sanctions, direct or indirect, which can be employed against a spouse who refuses to obey the order, which usually becomes a dead letter.

The Settlement of Matrimonial Disputes

Of course, not every broken marriage ends up in court, whether on a petition for divorce or for any other form of relief. Sometimes the parties will simply be content to separate on an informal basis, either because they have no choice, in that neither has given the other grounds for divorce, or because neither wishes to seek any formal remedy. In these cases, as well as in those where the parties have not encountered problems sufficiently serious to cause total breakdown, the law will not intervene. The parties are perfectly free to come to their own arrangements regarding future performance of family obligations and future enjoyment of family property now that the latter can no longer be used by all. Unfortunately, however, human nature being what it is, the breakdown of a marriage frequently leaves the parties in a state of embitterment towards each other which is not conducive towards the amicable settlement of their affairs. Thus, disputes often arise about the division of family property, custody of and access towards children and mutual financial obligations—to mention only three of the commonest causes of dissension. Where matrimonial breakdown has resulted in one spouse bringing a petition for matrimonial relief, such matters will most commonly be dealt with at the same time as the petition, but otherwise any dispute will have to be resolved independently. So family law has to provide machinery for the settlement of disputes of this kind in a manner which ensures justice to the parties and at the same time endeavours to secure that the family as a whole continues to be adequately provided for.

i. Division of Family Property. To take the problem of division of family property first, this is frequently the most serious bone of contention between the parties. It may be relatively easy for them to come to some form of agreement about the children and their maintenance, but the division of the family home and its contents may produce endless bitter arguments. Part of the trouble lies in the fact that in this particular sphere the law does not cater as imaginatively as perhaps it might for the realities of family life. The law is indeed clear in principle. In this country marriage does not result in any form of merger of the parties' property, and any property acquired by the spouses after marriage belongs to whichever one of them supplied the purchase price. The difficulty is to apply these basically simple principles, whereby the law regards the matrimonial home and its contents like any other piece of property and ascribes ownership to the purchaser, to the actual situation in the vast majority of families. Today the tendency is for boys and girls to marry at an ever-younger age, and it naturally follows that an overwhelmingly high proportion of them have little or nothing in the way of money or possessions when they marry. Thus, if the marriage should founder at a later date most of what then constitutes family property has been acquired subsequent to the marriage, and usually by the joint efforts of both spouses. This situation would not in itself produce serious problems if it were usual for husbands and wives to come to some agreement about the ownership of what has been acquired and its division in the event of a marriage breakdown. All that the law would then have to do would be to ensure that at the time of breakdown each party was held to his or her former agreement. However, at a time when all is well between them few spouses indeed can be induced to contemplate the break-up of their marriage, even in the confines of a solicitor's office, and few would consider taking legal advice at all. The result is that the break-up of a marriage usually presents a lawyer with a seemingly inextricable problem of sorting out the ownership of property which has been acquired by the efforts and financial contributions of both spouses in differing but unascertainable proportions. The problem arises so frequently that our law has been compelled to provide a solution, but one which, it is feared, may often produce injustice.

When a spouse raises the question of division of family property while applying for matrimonial relief he or she may well be able to succeed in obtaining an order for the transference of the whole or some part of the other's share according to the justice of the case and having regard to the responsibility of each for the breakdown of the marriage. In this respect the Court can make an order which will not depend upon strict rights of ownership. However, where the dispute about family property does not arise in the context of a petition for matrimonial relief the Court has no power to deprive a spouse of property which is his, despite the fact that he may be largely, or even wholly, responsible for the failure of the marriage. Here, therefore, there is nothing for it but the Court must attempt to divide up the family home and its contents in accordance with such rights of ownership as each is able to establish. The law is acutely conscious of the injustice which this not infrequently does to the spouse, usually the wife, whose financial contributions towards the home may have been little or nothing, but who may yet have contributed a great deal over the years in kind. Wherever possible the Court will divide on an equal basis, and this will be the inevitable result where the parties have merged their resources and the disputed property was purchased from this common fund. The husband will not then gain a greater share than the wife merely because it is obvious that he has contributed considerably more than she has to the common fund. However, the conscientious and industrious housewife who has not contributed anything directly towards the home and its contents may be in an invidious position. Her rights may then depend wholly on whether she can show that she and her husband had agreed to share whatever was acquired by their joint efforts. Such an agreement is hard to prove, for clearly most couples regulate their daily lives upon tacit rather than express assumptions. Whatever the position, however, it will obviously be to both parties' advantage to put bitterness aside and come to some agreement about division of family property, for, although the house itself may not have depreciated, any sum realised by an enforced sale of the contents will be a miserably inadequate substitute for the right to enjoy the use of the goods themselves. Sometimes it is possible for the Court to encourage agreement and at the same time do justice to a wife who has little to which she can lay claim in law by reducing the husband's continuing maintenance obligations if he will agree to allow the wife to continue to enjoy the use of family property.

ii. Financial Support of the Family. Mutual rights and obligations of support also loom large in most marriage breakdowns. While the spouses are living together on more or less amicable terms it will be for them to arrange among themselves the role of each in the life of the family. There is nothing in the law which compels the spouses to adopt the traditional roles of male-breadwinner and female-housewife, and if, as is becoming increasingly common, they agree each to share both tasks, or even that the roles should be wholly reversed, the Court will, if breakdown occurs, pay regard to the former position in regulating what the obligations of each concerning finance are to be in the future. Nevertheless, the law is framed in general terms to deal with the majority situation, which is that the husband shoulders the burden of providing for the family financially, while the wife has the task of ensuring that the money which she receives from her husband is duly used to supply the family's daily needs. If the marriage breaks down the law must ensure that these functions are continued, albeit in a radically altered setting. As far as concerns responsibility for infant children, the law is simple. Both spouses are obliged to support them financially, although, as is only to be expected, the wife's obligation is frequently one which she is unable to fulfil, and, in the case of young children, it is usually one which it would be undesirable for her to undertake. Thus, a husband is compelled by law to support his infant children, whether they are in his wife's care or his own, and this obligation is a very real one in practice. Whether or not the wife's obligation is, practically speaking, a real one will depend upon the circumstances of each individual case. Young children will usually be delivered into the wife's care on break-up of the marriage, and the husband can then be ordered to support them whether or not the breakdown leads to divorce. Questions of responsibility for the breakdown of the marriage may play a part in determining which of the spouses obtains custody of the children thereafter, but they in no way affect the spouses' financial duties. Thus, a so-called guilty wife who has custody of her infant children can obtain maintenance for them from her husband whether or not he has divorced her, and the converse is likewise true, although rare from a practical point of view.

Questions of guilt or innocence are, however, of far greater importance when dealing with the spouses' rights of support against each other. A husband who obtains matrimonial relief against his wife may not have to support her at all, and even if she does induce the Court to make an order in her favour, the amount of maintenance ordered will depend to a great extent on the degree of misconduct of which she is guilty. Where the wife is the petitioner and obtains relief against the husband, any misconduct on her part will also be taken into account by the Court when fixing maintenance. If no matrimonial relief is sought by either spouse a wife who is guilty of a matrimonial offence may find herself totally without rights of support against her husband, even though he may be equally guilty. The same principles hold good in the case of a husband petitioning for maintenance against his wife, although here even an innocent husband has very limited rights against his wife. A wife may be ordered to support a husband whom she has divorced, or against whom she has obtained a decree of judicial separation, on the ground of his incurable insanity, but other than this the Court is not in general empowered to grant maintenance to an innocent husband in a suit for matrimonial relief. If the husband does not seek matrimonial relief he may obtain a limited amount of maintenance from his wife from the Magistrates' Courts, but only if he is incapable of maintaining himself by reason of age, illness or other disability. Naturally, even this limited right may prove ineffectual practically speaking against a wife who is unable to earn more than is sufficient to support herself and her children.

iii. Custody of Children. Disputes over custody of and access to children of the family must be considered in the light of the general law relating to child welfare, for the breakdown of a marriage is by no means the only situation which gives rise to problems regarding the future care and upbringing of children. The State has always had an overriding duty to protect the nation's infant children, and for this reason, although the Courts are usually only too thankful to find that husbands and wives have been able to settle their differences among themselves, any private agreement relating to the children of the family will not necessarily be implemented. One of the most celebrated, and certainly one of the most important statutory provisions in the entire field of family law is section 1 of the Guardianship of Infants Act, 1925. This section is framed in the widest possible terms, and its essential effect is that where in any proceeding before any court the custody or upbringing of an infant is in question the Court shall regard the welfare of the infant as the first and paramount consideration. It follows, therefore, that no agreement which attempts to provide for the custody or upbringing of an infant will be enforced unless it is consistent with the infant's welfare so to do. As has already been stated, the general rule is that no judge may grant matrimonial relief in respect of a broken marriage unless he is satisfied that the parties have made proper arrangements for the future care and upbringing of every child of the family under sixteen. This provision effectively ensures that where the husband–wife relationship is dissolved the obligations implicit in the parent–child relationship will continue to be performed. Disputes between husband and wife as to mutual rights of custody and access will be resolved in accordance with the child's best interests, and other factors, such as the conduct of the parents *vis-à-vis* each other, can never be allowed to override this primary consideration.

Where a marriage has broken down and no matrimonial relief is sought by either party, there are numerous ways in which questions of care and upbringing can be brought before the courts if necessary. For example, it may be possible to have the children's future adjudicated upon on a complaint to the Magistrates' Court or to the High Court that one spouse has been guilty of matrimonial misconduct, or simply that there has been a wilful failure to provide financial support for the other spouse or children. If there is no question of misconduct a petition for custody can be brought by either spouse to either the Magistrates' Court, the County Court or the High Court. If the dispute is confined to a particular issue, such as the child's education or the proper administration of a fund to which the child is entitled, then the correct mode of procedure would be to seek the directions of the Chancery Division of the High Court by making the child a ward of court.

The obligations comprised in the relationship of parent and child in no way depend upon questions of legitimacy. A child is legitimate in English law if it is conceived or born in lawful wedlock, although a subsequent decree of nullity of marriage will not usually affect the status of the child. A child may also be legitimated by the subsequent marriage of his parents, and thereafter his legal position is substantially the same as if he had been born in lawful wedlock. However, neither legitimacy nor legitimation determine the extent of parental obligations. A mother is bound to maintain her illegitimate child, and so also is the man whom the Court may adjudge to be the father (called in law, the putative father). But quite apart from these latter obligations which have nothing to do with marital obligations as such, the bond of marriage may well cause the relationship of parent and child to come into being in the sense that the responsibilities of that relationship are present, but without the physical tie of parenthood. So, a husband or wife may accept a child of the other spouse as a member of the family, and the subsequent breakdown of the marriage might well involve the step-parent in financial liability for that child's future care and upbringing. In making any financial award against the step-parent, however, the court will have regard to the extent to which responsibility for the child was assumed and also to whether or not there is some third person, such as a former husband or wife of the other spouse, who is liable to maintain the child.

State Responsibilities in the Field of Child Welfare

At the commencement of this chapter it was stated that one of the most important functions of family law was to ensure that all members of the family were adequately provided for if and when the family should cease to function in the normal way, whether by reason of misfortune or misconduct. Until now we have been considering only how the law seeks to compel the parties to carry out their family duties, but clearly there are many occasions when the break-up of a family or the breakdown of a marriage leaves the members in need. The real victims of family or marriage breakdowns are the children, and where there is no one who is legally responsible for them or no one who, even if responsible, is capable of looking after them, then the State must assume their care. The State performs this function through the medium of local government, and the powers and duties of local authorities in regard to orphaned, abandoned or neglected children are numerous. In the case of orphaned children or children whose sole parent is incapable or unwilling to continue care (e.g. an unmarried mother or widowed father), it may be possible to arrange adoption into another family unit. In the case of very young children, adoption is clearly the most desirable solution, and every year local authorities and registered adoption societies are instrumental in bringing about thousands of successful adoptions. Elaborate safeguards exist to ensure that the adoption will be in the child's best interests, and although the general rule is that no order can be made without the consent of the child's natural parent or parents, it may be possible for the Court to dispense with consent if satisfied that the adoption should take place. Broadly speaking, consent can be dispensed with if the parent has persistently neglected his parental responsibilities or is withholding consent unreasonably. An example of unreasonable withholding of consent would be a refusal purely because the identity of the prospective adopters had not been disclosed.

Where adoption is not desirable or practical, the children's department of the local authority must receive children in need into its care and will either look after them in institutions or board them out with foster-parents. Wherever possible, the latter course will be chosen, as home care is preferable to that which can be provided by an institution, however kindly and humanely administered. Sometimes a local authority will be required to intervene in situations of temporary emergency where there has been no breakdown of either of the two constituent family relationships but where the parents find themselves suddenly unable to provide proper care for their children. A common example of this is loss of house accommodation. Where the child's need is likely to be permanent, the local authority can assume parental rights over it, but this can be done in face of parental opposition only if the parent has either abandoned the child, or is unfit to retain care, or is suffering from a permanent disability which renders him incapable of looking after the child. The circumstances in which local-authority action may be initiated vary a great deal. Sometimes it is the parents themselves who seek assistance, as would be the case where a family is suddenly rendered homeless; sometimes the police will discover a child whose circumstances need investigation, subsequently leading to assumption of care; sometimes doctors or hospitals will notify a local authority that its services are needed and so on. The Courts, too, will play their part in a variety of ways. For example, both the Magistrates' Courts and the High Court have power in matrimonial disputes to place children in the care of, or under the supervision of, a local authority. And in an entirely different type of situation a Juvenile Court, or other court adjudicating upon a criminal charge, may decide that a child involved in the case needs to be taken into care. If a child is himself brought before the Juvenile Court on a criminal charge one of the ways of dealing with him may be to make a 'fit person' order. This gives the 'fit person', who is usually the children's officer of a local authority, parental rights so long as the order is in force, and may result in a child being removed from undesirable home conditions.

However, although the State must and does provide for the care of children in need, the law recognises that a child requires more than the basic necessities of life to enable it to develop into a responsible, healthy adult. The emotional ties of parent and child count for much in this latter respect, and wherever possible the law encourages the continuation of the normal parent–child relationship. Thus, where a child is taken into care because of some temporary family emergency, the parents are not permitted to abnegate their responsibilities, and local authorities must endeavour to ensure that a parent or some other near relative resumes care as soon as practicable. Only if satisfied that it will not be in the child's interests to reunite him with his former connections will a local authority assume more permanent control. In this way the law fills the gap left by failure of parental care but does all that it can to ensure that the parents themselves continue to fulfil the obligations which the fact of parenthood has imposed upon them.

For the future, the hardest problem which family lawyers will have to face and solve is how to retain a proper balance between what are perhaps two basically conflicting objectives, namely, ensuring that the duties consequent upon the husband–wife and parent–child relationships continue to be performed, while at the same time giving way to society in its ever-increasing desire for more individual liberty in the formation and dissolution of those relationships. There are those who claim that the changes which this century has seen in the structure of family life, such as the recognition of equality of status between husband and wife and the modern phenomenon of the working mother, have already considerably weakened the strength of family life in England. They argue that any further relaxation of the law, such as would be occasioned by the introduction of easier divorce, cannot but result in irreparable harm, particularly in the field of child welfare. Others, while admitting the possibility that family ties may not be as strong as they were, see no alternative but to react to public opinion in whichever way it should develop. Certainly our efforts to educate the community to meet the challenge of family life need to be improved, and there is a strong case for introducing formal education on these lines into school curricula. But much will depend on the success or failure of family law in fostering the necessary sense of family responsibility by wise processes of development.

Suggested Reading

E. L. JOHNSON, *Family Law*, Sweet & Maxwell.
T. E. JAMES, *Child Law*, Sweet & Maxwell.
Putting Asunder, S.P.C.K.
The Field of Choice, The Law Commission—Reform of the Grounds of Divorce. Cmnd. 3123.
R. H. GRAVESON and F. R. CRANE, ed., *A Century of Family Law*, Sweet & Maxwell.

NOTES

[1] The Law Commission set up by the present Government will be treating the further development of family law as a matter of high priority. It is understood that over the course of the next few years radical changes may be expected in almost every aspect of this field. This does not, of course, indicate that our present laws are wholly misconceived, but only that the rapidly changing social context in which they operate requires that this subject, of all others, be constantly under review. It will be appreciated that the writer of this chapter can do no more than survey the law as it exists at the moment of writing.

[2] The word 'infant' is here used in its legal sense, thus signifying a person under the age of 21, the present age of majority.

[3] See *Hyde* v. *Hyde and Woodmansee* (1866) L.R. 1 P. & D. 130 at p. 133.

[4] Contained in the Marriage Act, 1949.

[5] The exception is wilful refusal to consummate the marriage which, by definition must indicate that the party refusing is sexually capable. It is thus a grievance which arises *after* the celebration of the marriage.

[6] The only court which at present has jurisdiction to grant matrimonial relief is the Probate Divorce and Admiralty Division of the High Court of Justice. A Bill which would give the County Courts jurisdiction to hear undefended divorce suits is on its way through Parliament at the time of going to press.

9

Property and Trusts

(A) LAND

R. H. Maudsley

General

A SYSTEM OF PROPERTY LAW must provide for society a framework within which owners of property may enjoy it in security, and dispose of it by conveyance or by will to strangers or to members of the family according to any reasonable desire they may have; consistently, of course, with the general habits and customs of the society in question. In a developed society, the landowner's freedom of enjoyment and disposition exists subject to far-reaching control imposed by the State in the public interest.

Inevitably, this produces a complicated system; one which lawyers must learn to handle even if laymen cannot. If English Land Law seems excessively technical—and much of the language of this branch of the law is far removed from everyday speech—this is because of the paramount need for certainty in property law. The property owner does not wish to take 'calculated risks' in making dispositions; rather, he wants to know what means of achieving his purpose the law puts at his disposal, and he wants to be sure that a disposition of a particular kind will have *exactly* the effect that it was expected to have. The desired degree of certainty can be accomplished only by paying the price of technicality.

In order to understand the way in which the English system of property owning works, it is necessary to go back to feudal times. The system of landholding which developed then is still the basis of modern land law. It is, of course, the modern law that we are trying to understand, and the story will be one of transition over several hundred years. Development comes sometimes by decided cases and sometimes, more particularly in recent years, by statute. The greatest statutory reforms came in 1925 in a series of statutes which made great changes in modernising the law. Reference will be made later to some of them.

The Feudal System

The feudal system was one in which interests in land were granted by the King to his supporters, who in turn would make grants of some of their land to other people. This process might continue until the persons in actual possession of the land were separated by several degrees from the King. Those who received their grant direct from the King were called Tenants-in-Chief, and, like all the other landholders, they would pay homage to the King as their feudal lord and perform other services. The King was thus the greatest feudal lord of them all, receiving homage and services and never paying, while the other landowners, apart from the ones at the very bottom, would both receive and pay.

The stability of the society of those days depended upon the maintenance of this structure of landholding, and the earliest actions in the King's court are those relating to the rights of the owners of freehold land to be reinstated in their holding. If the security of freehold landholding had disappeared feudal society would have collapsed.

It will be seen that several persons were in some way concerned with any one particular piece of land. A most important consequence of this fact was that the question, Who Owned It? was not answerable at all under the feudal law. A mere tenant could hardly be called the owner. Later the lawyers said that the King owned all the land. The fact remained however, that the King's ownership was, in a great many cases, purely nominal, and added nothing to his rights as feudal lord of the tenants-in-chief. Moreover, the tenants-in-chief, in turn, had practically the same rights over their own tenants by virtue of the lord–tenant relationship.

We find, therefore, that most of the rights and obligations of the land 'owner' in early law were expressed in terms of tenure, i.e. the lord–tenant relationship, but there was one vital aspect of landowning which the theory of tenure did not encompass, namely the *duration* of the relationship. In the earliest days a feudal lord would naturally wish to have as tenants persons whom he had selected and could rely upon, and so a grant of land would be made only for the life of the tenant. As the element of personal trust soon lost most of its importance, the practice grew up of granting land to be held by the tenant during his lifetime, and then, after the tenant's death, by his heir, then by the heir's heir and so on until the holder of the land for the time being died without there being anyone to succeed to it.

Clearly there is a great practical difference between a tenure which lasts only one lifetime and a tenure which, potentially at any rate, can exist for ever. As this difference was not capable of being expressed in terms of the theory of tenure, the lawyers of the feudal period invented a new concept—that of 'estates'. The estate describes the duration of the tenant's interest in the land, and the tenant is said to be the owner of his estate, thereby providing English law with a highly original solution to the analytical difficulties of ownership of land.

Because the original impulse for the development of the doctrine of estates was given by the recognition of inheritance of land, the various types of estate were defined by reference not to the calendar but to the classes of heirs who could succeed to the land. On this basis the following estates can be distinguished:

(*a*) Estate in Fee Simple. This was the greatest estate known to the law, for it would descend to any heirs whether lineal or collateral, and was capable of lasting for ever. It could be disposed of by the owner during his life, and would then last as long as the purchaser had heirs.

(*b*) Estate in Fee Tail. This estate would descend to the lineal heirs of the estate owner only. In theory it could not be disposed of by the owner, but ways were found by which an estate tail could be converted into an estate in fee simple and could be disposed of as such. This was technically termed Barring the Entail.

(*c*) Life Estate or Estate for the Life of Another.

These, then, were the freehold estates known to the common law. A grant of land was a grant of such an estate, and similarly a sale was the sale of such an estate. This aspect of English land law continues to this day, and a conveyance of land is technically still a conveyance not of land but of an estate in the land.

More than one estate could exist in the same land. Thus, if a life estate is given by X to A it is possible to give a fee simple after A's death to B. We would say that the land was given to A for life, remainder to B in fee simple. Similarly, if X as fee-simple owner granted only a life estate to A, X retained the fee simple and we would then say that X had a reversion. To sell 'the land'—by which we mean the whole fee-simple estate in the land—it was necessary at common law to transfer, in the one case, A's life estate and B's fee-simple remainder, and in the other case A's life estate and X's reversion. It was the responsibility of the purchaser to satisfy himself that he was buying estates from the people who owned them; and, also, that however many separate estates there may be, they always added up to the estate in the land which he proposed to purchase.

In addition to these 'freehold' estates, defined by lives and inheritance, the law recognised an estate limited for a fixed period of years. This was known as a Term of Years and was a 'leasehold' estate, that is to say, not only the estate but also the tenure is different. Owners of leasehold estates never fitted into the feudal system, and until about the year 1600 they were not given the protection which was necessarily given to the holders of freehold states. The lessee, or termor, as an owner of a term of years was called, could not specifically recover his estate if he were dis-

K   139

possessed; he had only a right of action for damages against the landlord, the freeholder. About the year 1600 leases became recoverable specifically in an action called Ejectment and have remained so to the present day. The early inability of the leaseholder to recover specifically his leasehold was significant, because specific recovery was the test to determine whether property was real or personal. Freehold estates were thus Real Property; leasehold estates were Personal Property. Until 1925 this distinction was of practical importance in various ways, the most significant being that they descended on intestacy according to quite different rules.

There was also a system of landholding known as Copyhold. This applied only to those on the lowest rung of the feudal ladder; it was abolished in 1925 and need not be further considered.

It will be seen that the important type of landholding in feudal times was freehold. The word tenant, when used in connection with feudal times, means a freeholder owning freehold land as tenant of his feudal lord. As feudal relationships have now disappeared, so has that use of the word; and it is now used to described the owner of a term of years, who holds the land of the freeholder by leasehold tenure.

Uses and Trusts

Thus far, this account has been restricted to *legal* estates in land, that is to say, those which were recognised by courts of law. Chapter 5 explained the jurisdiction of Courts of Equity and said something about the interests in property which were developed in Chancery. As would be expected, most of the development in the earliest days was connected with land and, in accordance with the usual policy, contained in the maxim that 'equity follows the law', the Court of Chancery recognised estates and interests in land which are, speaking generally, the same as those in existence at law.

For various reasons said to be connected with the fact of

landowners' going abroad to fight in the Crusades, and also with the problems arising from the fact that some monastic orders could not own land, the practice developed of conveying land to grantees who would hold 'to the use of' the grantor or some third person. The grantee was known as the feoffee to uses, and the person to whom the land was held the *cestui* (pronounced 'setty') *que use*. As explained above, the interests which the *cestui que use* could enjoy were similar to the legal estate in land which have been described.

Once this system had begun, it soon became clear that it had many advantages to landholders. For example, feudal dues were payable on the happening of certain events, notably on the death of the tenant and succession to the land by his heir; if the heir was an infant the lord had further valuable rights until the infant came of age. Some or all of these burdens could be avoided by arranging for the land to be held by a group of feoffees who would not die together and were not infants—an elementary form of tax avoidance. Moreover, by conveying the land to uses, the freeholder could evade certain common law restrictions on the way in which he could dispose of the land: in particular, he could make a will of the land (which was not possible at common law until 1540) and more elaborate family settlements. The only drawback was that uses gave the beneficiaries merely equitable interests, which were slightly less secure than legal interests, because of the Chancellor's refusal to enforce the use against a purchaser who took the land for value and without notice of the equitable interest.

The Statute of Uses

The avoidance of feudal dues was to the advantage of everybody except the King, who was, of course, under the feudal system always a receiver and never a payer. This was the main reason why Henry VIII persuaded Parliament to pass the Statute of Uses in 1535 with the intent of putting uses to an end for ever, by enacting that where land was held by one person to the use of another the legal estate in the land should be in that other.

The effect of the statute was partial and temporary. It was held not to apply to certain uses, and by the end of the seventeenth century conveyancers avoided the statute by inserting an additional use and relying on the statute to execute the first use; thus, instead of making conveyance to B to the use of C, the conveyance was drafted so as to convey to A to the use of B to the use of C: the use to C would previously have been regarded as repugnant to the use of B, and hence ineffective; but the political and economic climate of the seventeenth century was greatly changed from that of Henry VIII's day. The landowners desired the return of equitable interests which arose again in the form of a use upon a use, and these interests were later called trusts. The terminology employed was that of a conveyance unto and to the use of B in trust for C. A curious by-product of the Statute of Uses was that it enabled conveyancers to achieve at law all the elaborate dispositions of land which had previously been possible only in equity; the subsequent history of uses is, indeed, an interesting example of the way in which lawyers of ingenuity can make a servant out of a provision in a statute intended to be their master.

It will be seen that in their developed form common law and equity gave to landholders a wide variety of interests which could be created out of land. The system was indeed too complex and needed to be simplified. In addition, the system contained one great disadvantage: the fact that according to the Doctrine of Estates the owner of an estate or interest at law or equity was the only person who could convey it unless special power were given to someone else to do so. Thus, a family settlement might include a number of life estates and remainders in addition to liens and charges and an ultimate reversion in fee simple. A purchaser wishing to buy 'the land'—by which is here meant the unencumbered fee simple—had to deal with every person who owned an interest under the settlement. This gave effective protection to the owners of those interests, but made conveyances complicated and uncertain, and in some cases

would make the land unsaleable. The great family settlements of the eighteenth and nineteenth centuries under-
lined this point. With the huge industrial and suburban
expansion of the nineteenth century it became all the more
important for land to be alienable and available for development. What was needed was a system which would
enable a purchaser to buy the fee-simple interest in land
which was subject to a family settlement without having to
deal with a large number of 'vendors', and which at the
time would preserve the value to the beneficiaries under the
settlement of the interests which they owned.

Conveyancing

Before we examine this question further, it will be useful
to say something in outline of the principles of conveyancing under English Land Law.

As explained above, buyers and sellers do not deal in
theory with the land but with estates in the land. Conveyancing, therefore, involves the creation and transfer of
estates, and the conveyancer's job is to know what is to be
done and how to do it.

Certain formalities are required for dealing with certain
types of estates or interests in land. Generally speaking, all
estates and interests in land may be disposed of by conveyance *inter vivos* or by will. A conveyance takes effect on
execution and a will on the testator's death; the formalities
required for these instruments differ.

A person claiming to be entitled to an estate or interest
in land must show that it has been created in his favour in
the proper manner; and when selling this estate or interest
must satisfy the purchaser that this is so. On the sale of a
legal estate in land, therefore, a purchaser will require to see
the deeds and other documents of title in order to satisfy
himself that the seller is the owner of the estate. Interests
which other persons may have in the land will be brought
to the purchaser's attention in various ways, perhaps by
mention in the deeds, perhaps by inspection of the property
and perhaps by the inclusion of such interests in the

Register of Land Charges set up in 1925 by the Land Charges Act.

This system is efficient only if the documents in question are correctly drafted and kept. Where the title is handled without the benefit of a lawyer's advice, difficulties and uncertainties are sure to arise. A much more efficient system is that of Registration of Title, under which estates and interests in land are registered on proof of ownership. New interests and transfers are included in the register as they occur. Some land in England is dealt with this way. Under the Land Registration Acts 1925–1966, there is power to extend the system of registration, and this provides for the registration of ownership on the next transfer. It would be too great an undertaking to register every interest in the whole of England at the present time. New countries have adopted some system of this sort when lands were first granted, and it seems reasonable to hope that a system of registration will be in operation throughout all England by the 1980s.

Settlements

The problem facing a purchaser who wishes to buy land subject to a family settlement was mentioned above and its solution postponed. The solution adopted by the Law of Property Act 1925 was that legal estates could exist in two forms only; that is, either as a fee simple absolute in possession or as terms of years absolute. All other interests in land could exist as equitable interests only. This means that whatever the title to land, and however complicated the beneficial interests, the purchaser can buy the freehold estate from the fee-simple owner and a term of years from the owner of the term of years. Special provision is made by the Settled Land Act 1925 for the equitable interests, which would otherwise be binding on him because he had notice of them, to be 'overreached'. This is a technical term which means that the equitable interests are lifted off the land and attached to the purchase money. A purchaser, therefore, who follows the correct procedure, can buy the fee simple absolute in possession and obtain it free from the beneficial interests; while the owners of these interests do not suffer by the sale because their interests in the land are now replaced by exactly the same interests in the purchase money. The question from their point of view is whether or not they wish to have the family capital invested in land or in money.

Restriction of the Settlor's Freedom of Choice

It was said earlier that a system of property law should permit an owner to dispose of his property to strangers or among members of his family according to any reasonable desire he may have. The usual wish is to provide for a widow and children, and sometimes to provide for more remote issue. In this context, two important points must be raised:

(*a*.) Originating from the days when future interests existed in legal estates, and the tying up of interests in the remote future complicated titles to land, a limit was placed upon the time at which a person could become entitled to an interest in the future. This was set by the Rule Against Perpetuities which said that an interest was void if it might possibly vest in the donee beyond a period of 21 years following the death of someone now alive. The basis of this period is to allow a gift to a member of one generation for his life and then to a member of the next generation on his majority: as 'to my son for life, and then to his son at 21'. My grandson is certain to attain the age of 21 within 21 years of his father's (my son's) death. By statute of 1964, a settlor may choose a period of 80 years if he wishes instead of that of life or lives in being plus 21 years.

(*b*.) With substantial estates, the dominant question is not the selection of the interests which the settlor wishes to create, but rather the impact of taxation upon property interests. Tax liability is imposed in certain known situations, and a settlor's legal advisers will draft his settlement in such a way as to minimise its liability to tax. Various techniques have been developed. This is no place to discuss them; but a study of settlements must always take the tax aspect into account.

Rights Over Other People's Land

Such, in outline, are the beneficial interests which the law recognises in land. It recognises also certain interests in other people's land. A right to enter another's land and to take away some part of it—turf, fish, etc.—is a profit à prendre. Other rights between neighbours, such as a right of way or a right to light, are called easements, and they must be enjoyed, not personally, but by virtue of being the owner of what is called the 'dominant land' and exercised over the 'servient land'. Again, it is possible, on the sale of land, for the purchaser to covenant not to use the land in certain ways; and such covenants, properly drafted, can impose a burden on that land in favour of land retained by the seller.

Mortgages

Any legally recognised interest in property may be used for the purpose of giving security for a loan. In such a situation the borrower creates a charge on, or interest in, the property in favour of the lender. If the borrower repays, in accordance with the terms of the agreement, the charge or interest is cancelled, and is in fact never called into action. But if the borrower cannot repay, the lender, instead of joining the other creditors to take a share of the borrower's insolvent estate, can proceed against the property charged and have it sold to pay off the debt. He is a secured creditor and can proceed against the property given as security. Of course, he must take care to ensure that the property is of a value at least equal to that of the debt, or he will only take his share with the unsecured or general creditors for the balance.

Freehold land is a particularly suitable form of property

for this purpose. It is permanent, not consumable, and retains a steady and perhaps increasing value more reliably than other forms of property. Land therefore is used commonly for raising secured loans, whether by an individual for the purpose of purchasing his house or by a real estate developer for commercial purposes. Charges are mainly of two types: either by a formal mortgage created by deed and known as a charge by way of legal mortgage; or by the deposit of the deeds of land with a bank to secure a loan, usually in the form of an overdraft on a bank account, taking effect as an equitable mortgage.

Commercial undertakings usually raise money by yet another method. It would be unsatisfactory for them to charge any specific land with the repayment of a debt; for they may wish to sell that land or to take down buildings. They usually create a charge, not upon an individual piece of land but upon the company's undertaking as a whole, by means of what is known as a debenture.

Public Control of Land

When the question of the use of land in the commercial sphere is considered, a host of new questions arise. By common law theory, a fee simple owner can do as he likes with his land—subject in feudal times to the performance of his feudal duties. Today his activities are closely controlled in the public interest. He must obtain permission to effect any change of user, and he is liable to have his land purchased at a valuation for certain public purposes without his consent. Again, a landlord may, at common law, give his tenant a notice to quit, the notice being of a length agreed by the parties or as laid down by law. At the expiration of the period the tenant must leave, and may take with him only certain fixtures which were affixed for trade, domestic or ornamental purposes. Today, special security of tenure is given to agricultural, commercial and domestic tenants by statutes which over-ride the agreement of the parties. The law contained in statutes such as these, and that of the Income Tax and Finance Acts, is the law which most particularly concerns owners of land at the present time. This legislation, however, has never destroyed the theoretical bases of landholding in English law; and a proper study of land law, ancient or modern, takes one back inexorably to the Franciscan Friars living on lands held to use, and to tenants in Knight Service paying homage to their feudal lords.

(B) PERSONAL PROPERTY

A. D. Hughes

THE ENGLISH LAW of personal property has always been very much the poor relation of the land law. The common lawyers of the Middle Ages had time and energy to spare in working out the implications of the fantastically complex land law, but hardly a thought for moveable property. The historical origins of the modern law of personal property form a motley, and somewhat unlikely, collection: actions in tort derived from trespass, a strong flavouring from the law of contract, a smattering of Roman law and a sizeable contribution from the Chancellors.

In this state of affairs it is not surprising that the law of personal property lacks coherence. Another disruptive influence is the diversity of 'objects' (using the word loosely) which go to make up the list of personal property. It is perfectly feasible to have a single method for transferring the legal rights to any piece of land—from this point of view all land is alike; but how can the same modes of transfer be appropriate for a gift of an inexpensive watch and an assignment of patent rights? All land can be possessed, and so can household furniture; but how do you possess a trade mark? In the account which follows we shall refer briefly to the more important types of personal property, and then consider the practical workings of ownership and possession in relation to the more everyday types.

What is Personal Property?

'Personal' is here opposed to 'real', and a useful working definition of personal property would be that it embraces all property rights except those in land. This is not historically exact, for a lease of land is technically personal property as we have seen, but this is an oddity which can be overlooked at the present day. However, we are still left with the difficult question 'What are property rights?' Without pretending to be wholly accurate, we can say that the marks of a property right are that it is *acquired* in some way, *exclusive* to a definite person or group of persons, *protected* against interference by any outside person *without the need to show a special duty* on that person not to interfere with the right, and (generally) *transferable*. By far the most important word in this definition is 'acquired', and much of the law of personal property is concerned with *how* you acquire the various interests, or rights, which the law permits. If I have validly acquired a car or a copyright I am said to have title (or 'good title') to it. Ownership is the commonest property right, but, just as in the case of land, it is not the only type of personal property right.

The primary objects of personal property rights are physical things, known technically as chattels (or 'chattels personal' to distinguish them from leases which are 'chattels real'). Physical objects are also known as 'choses [or 'things'] in possession' to distinguish them from the other broad category of personal property—intangible rights—which are called 'choses [or 'things'] in action'. These two names are derived from the fact that in the case of objects having a physical existence you can assert your rights to them by taking possession of them, whereas your claim to an intangible right can only be asserted by bringing an action. Shares and other company securities, negotiable instruments, patents, trade marks and copyrights are all choses in action and personal property. The modern law on all these subjects is almost entirely statutory and highly specialised; the discussion of the law of personal property which follows refers only to 'things in possession'.

Ownership in Relation to Personal Property

The law of personal property is not burdened by doctrines of tenure and estates. There are no degrees of ownership in chattels: either I am the owner of 'my' car or I am not. If I am not the owner, somebody else is (for example, a hire-purchase finance company), unless the car (or other object) has been abandoned, when there would be no owner of it at all. There is no question of my being a life tenant, or even a lessee (though hire agreements can be drawn to approximate very closely to leases, with the important difference that a lease is binding on third parties and a hiring agreement is not). Of course there is a resulting loss of flexibility, but this is not a serious matter, for by the use of the trust the owner of personal property can achieve everything he requires in the way of settlements.

There are two main methods of acquiring ownership of chattels: by sale (that is, in return for value given), and by gift. As might be expected, the requirements for the acquisition of ownership gratuitously are somewhat more stringent than in the other case, and we will look first at these. A gift will only operate as a transfer of the donor's ownership if it is made by a writing under seal or the object of the gift is delivered to the donee, that is, put into his possession. Even if the former method is used, delivery will also normally be made at the earliest opportunity, for otherwise the donee's position may be prejudiced unless the document has been registered under the Bills of Sale Acts.

Basically, delivery is effected by a physical handing over of the object, but in many instances the law accepts other acts as an adequate substitute for handing over. If the object is too heavy or too large to move by hand delivery is made by putting the donee in sole control or enjoyment of it, for example, in the case of a car, by handing over the keys. Alternatively, the donor may make 'symbolic' delivery, for example, by handing over a kitchen chair as a 'symbol' of all the furniture in the house, or by putting his hand on the grand piano and saying 'This is now yours.' If the donee is already in possession at the time of the gift, because, for example, the object had been lent to him by the donor, there is no need for the pantomime of symbolic delivery, and the gift is complete on the strength of the donor's words of gift alone.

You cannot force a gift upon the donee; on the other hand, no formal acceptance by him is necessary, so that a gift made without the donee's knowledge is provisionally valid, and will only fail if, on learning of it, the donee repudiates the gift. A gift once made is irrevocable except on certain clearly defined grounds. Fraud, misrepresentation, coercion and abuse by the donee of a position of confidence or authority over the donor (a real possibility in the case of gifts by child to parent, client to solicitor) are grounds for rescinding a gift—ingratitude by the donee and second thoughts by the donor are not.

Gifts in the popular sense are not the only cause of gratuitous transfer of ownership. The death of the owner naturally involves the transfer of all his assets to other persons. Some will be sold by the executor of the will (or by the administrator of the estate if the owner died 'intestate', i.e. without leaving a valid will) to pay expenses, taxes and debts; a large part of the remainder will probably be sold and the proceeds used to pay legacies, or the shares of the next of kin on intestacy, but there are also occasions when specific assets will pass to the successors of the deceased. Such successors will then acquire ownership by delivery from the executor or the administrator.

The effect of a transfer *for value* differs in two most important respects from that of a gratuitous transfer. In the first place, as we have seen in Chapter 6, ownership passes from seller to buyer, *not* when the goods are delivered *but when the parties agree that it shall pass*. It is perfectly possible for the ownership to change, although the goods have never left the seller's possession. In practice, however, the buyer who obtains ownership under the terms of agreement, without getting possession of the goods, has his ownership rendered far less secure than ownership with possession would be, by virtue of the principles next mentioned.

Secondly, although a gift can never operate to transfer to the donee a better right to the goods than the donor had, a sale can do just this. If A is in possession of B's car without B's consent, and makes a gift of the car to C, C will not acquire ownership for the simple reason that A had no ownership to transfer. If the situation is the same, except that A *sells* the car to C (who is in good faith and has no knowledge of B's rights in the car), the same answer *could* be given, but it is not so obviously the appropriate answer. The law has to weigh the need for security in commercial transactions, when decisions must often be taken on a basis of trust and in reliance on the appearance of ownership, against the desire for security and indefeasibility of property rights. In the example given it would be just as hard on C for him to lose his money when he had no reason to distrust A as it would be hard on B if he should lose his car because A sold something he had no right to sell.

Traditionally, the rule of the common law was to protect B, the original owner, against C, the innocent purchaser for value, by allowing B to recover the car, or its value, from C, and leaving C to whatever remedy he might have against A. This rule is commonly expressed in the Latin maxim '*Nemo dat quod non habet*' ('No one can give what he does not have'). Gradually, however, a series of exceptions to the rule was introduced in the nineteenth century, most of which are today collected in the Sale of Goods Act, 1893. The most important exceptions, where a sale by A (who has no right to sell) will confer a good title on C (who is in good faith and has no notice of A's lack of title) and defeat the claim of the original owner (B), are the following. First, if A is a 'mercantile agent' and the sale to C is in the ordinary course of A's business, C obtains a good title so long as the original owner consented to A's possession of the goods (although he did not consent to A's selling them). Secondly, if B the owner is 'estopped', that is, precluded by his conduct from denying that A had the right to sell, C obtains a good title. This is a particular application of the principle discussed earlier in connection with the law of agency (see Chapter 6) that a person who creates the appearance of authority to act on his behalf cannot deny the existence of the authority to the prejudice of those who have relied on the appearance. Thirdly, if A had a voidable title to the goods, and his title had not been avoided at the time of the sale to C, C obtains a good title. A voidable title is one which is provisionally valid, but is liable to be set aside, on the ground, for example, of fraud. Such a situation would arise where B agrees to sell his car to A, and accepts A's cheque in payment, but the cheque is worthless. B has the right to avoid (i.e. cancel) the sale but he must do so *before* A sells the car to an innocent purchaser. Fourthly, if the owner of goods sells them, first, to X and remains in possession after the sale, sale and *delivery* of the same goods to Y will defeat X's ownership under the first sale, provided, of course, that Y was in good faith and had no notice of the sale to X. Conversely, if the buyer of goods obtains possession of them with the seller's consent, even though there is a term of the contract that the ownership of the goods shall remain in the seller (because, for example, the price has not yet been paid), the buyer can pass a good title to the goods to an innocent third-party purchaser.

This last provision was deprived of much of its usefulness by a decision of the House of Lords given soon after the Sale of Goods Act was passed, which excluded the hire-purchaser from the list of 'buyers'. Many innocent purchasers, particularly of cars, were caught out by the fact that the goods were only held by the seller on hire-purchase, so that he had no right to sell them at all. This gap in the law was, however, plugged for most purposes by the Hire Purchase Act, 1964.

Possession

No account of the law of personal property could be complete without some reference, however brief, to the part played by possession. We have already seen how important the taking of possession is to the donee and to the buyer. The fact of taking possession, without more, confers ownership of things previously without an owner, such as abandoned objects and (subject to the game laws) wild animals. Even if the object of which you take possession does have an owner, your possession gives you a claim to it which is subject only to the claim of the owner; if he cannot be found, or if he does not assert his claim, your possession is indistinguishable from ownership. The most common illustration of this is in connection with the finding of lost articles. 'Finders Keepers' is not a maxim of the law, and indeed the actual finder is usually defeated by the fact that the article was on some person's land, and hence, in that person's possession at the time of finding, but the principle remains that the first *possessor* has the best right after the owner, and has full right except as against the owner.

In the same way the 'Bailee' of goods—the person who has received possession of the goods on the terms of some agreement with the owner, whether it is a contract of carriage, storage, loan, hire or whatever—is as fully protected against wrongful interference with his possession as the owner himself. Even the thief is a possessor, and (in theory at any rate) enjoys the same full protection.

Suggested Reading

A. LAND

A. D. HARGREAVES, *An Introduction to the Principles of Land Law*, Sweet & Maxwell.

B. PERSONAL PROPERTY

J. CROSSLEY VAINES, *Personal Property*, Butterworths.
T. A. BLANCO WHITE, *Industrial Property and Copyright*, Stevens.

10

International Law

(A) PUBLIC INTERNATIONAL LAW

G. I. A. D. Draper

Its Nature, Background and Sources

BY PUBLIC INTERNATIONAL LAW (here referred to simply as international law) is meant that body of principles and rules of conduct which bind states in their relations with each other. If international law is properly to be considered as law it must partake of the essential features of all law. Likewise, it can be considered as law if no viable definition of law can exclude it. It is thought that the essential conditions for all law are the existence of a political community and the acceptance by its members that there are rules of conduct binding on them as such.

The unique quality of international law is that it is primarily, but not exclusively, a body of rules binding states. A state is a form of institution characterised by its power and its paramountcy. An institution, in its turn, is a network of relationships between men who are associated together for a common purpose. In fact, states exist and they operate, consciously, as members of a community of states.

The modern territorial state is a development of the last four hundred years, arising out of the break up of medieval Christendom and Empire. International law in the modern sense has evolved during that period, although some earlier symptoms can be seen in ancient societies, such as that of ancient Greece. The Greek city states, sharing a common culture and religion and being independent of each other, could and did generate a system of inter-city relationships influenced by rules and treaties.

The Middle Ages, although producing some useful ideas for modern international law, such as a 'natural law' binding all creation, retarded its appearance to the extent that the independent territorial state was not part of, but alien to, the medieval system in Europe. Feudalism and the divided power of Prince and Church were factors dissuasive of the rise of modern international law. The Reformation broke up the medieval structure and led to the emergence of the territorial state, master of its own affairs and independent of other states.

Obviously, some rules were needed for the governing of relations between these states, if chaos was to be avoided. The need and the age produced the men. One such was Grotius, a Netherlander of prodigious abilities, who wrote his great and influential treatise on *The Law of War and Peace* in 1625. This was the first systematic exposition of a law of nations, consisting of rules designed to govern the conduct of states in their mutual relations. Grotius stressed that states should see themselves as members of a society.

During the seventeenth and eighteenth centuries the practice of states evolved a body of customary rules which were supplemented by writers. State treaty practice also contributed to the law of nations. There was particular development in the customary law of war and neutrality, and, more specifically, in the law of war and neutrality at sea. In the nineteenth century treaty law was in the ascendancy. In the latter half of it multilateral treaties were concluded designed to codify the customary law of war, the first part of the law of nations to receive this treatment. Even by the end of the nineteenth century international law was primarily the law between European states sharing a common Christian culture and history.

Until the twentieth century the international community of states was very loose, reflecting the comparative weakness of the law of nations. Its very basis was permanently exposed to disruption by the place that war held in international law.

A somewhat closer knit international community, with a reduced recognition of the place of war, was attempted in the Covenant of the League of Nations of 1920. Even then the League was very much a European organisation. In 1945 the international community was made a tighter and wider system by the establishment of the Charter of the United Nations. This Charter created the United Nations Organisation, which now comprises 121 Member States.

From where does international law derive? Grotius and the other early writers had borrowed heavily from Roman Law, accepted in the Middle Ages as 'written reason', from 'natural law' ideas and from the Scriptures. The practices and usages of states had hardened, by their general acceptance, into customary rules. Such rules are considered to be binding when States act as if they were so binding, and accept that unpleasant consequence will attend their violation in circumstances that afford the violating state no ground for complaint against other states. Today the Statute of the International Court of Justice, appended to and part of the Charter of the United Nations, is normally regarded as specifying authoritatively the sources of modern international law. This Statute has been accepted by all the 121 Member States of the United Nations and by those non-Members who invoke the Court's jurisdiction. The Statute directs the Court, whose function it is to decide cases according to international law, to apply: (i) international conventions (treaties); (ii) international custom; (iii) general principles of law recognised by civilised nations; and (iv) judicial decisions and the writings of leading jurists, described as 'subsidiary means for the determination of rules of law'. The 'general principles' are those which mature legal systems incorporate as intrinsically reasonable and advantageous for furthering order and justice.

In spite of the theoretical difficulties writers have advanced for the subjection of sovereign states to the yoke of law, states themselves consider that international law does bind them and have given expression to that fact in Article

1 (1) of the Charter of the United Nations. The existence of states presents no essential contradiction to the idea of legal subjection, but their power presents difficulties in the way of regular and consistent enforcement of that law. That is a separate matter and an experience which state (municipal) law has had to meet and resolve when confronted with certain powerful elements within the state.

The Topics of International Law

The great expansion of the scope and content of international law is a phenomenon of our times. It is the necessary corollary to the widening state co-operation and the establishment of innumerable international institutions established for that purpose. These latter operate ever more actively in the spheres of transport, economic and social development, communications, scientific advance, health and education. These trends have added considerably to the delineaments of international law now to be described.

i. States. Primarily, international law is concerned with states. Hence the law about states occupies a central place in international law. It is still based upon the acceptance of the sovereignty and equality of states, as can be seen in Article 2 (1) of the Charter of the United Nations. The Organisation is based on the principle of the sovereign equality of all its Members. States are the terminal points of international relationships. They are the repositories, or subjects, of the rights and duties which determine the precise content of those relationships. Thus international law seeks to identify states, to tell us how and when they come into existence and disappear, what they can and cannot do in relation to other states and what their duties are. It considers that the essential attributes of a state are a discernible territory, a people having some nexus with that territory, and a government which operates effectively in that territory and is independent of any external control by other states.

The states of Europe grew up with international law. They were the founder members of the international community. International law was evolved to harmonise and control their relations with each other. Later, the question arose how other and new states were to be admitted to this community. Must they be recognised if they display the attributes already mentioned, who must recognise them and on what conditions? The field of recognition is one of the least satisfactory parts of our present international law, and the current ideological divisions in the world have done little to improve the situation. The law knows of no authoritative body which can determine the recognition of states or governments. The United Nations has no competence in that direction. The controversy has ranged over whether states come into legal being only by the act of recognition from other states, or by the fact of their existence which other states must determine as best they can in the light of their own judgment. Some states, such as the United Kingdom, consider that recognition should be determined by the presence or absence of objective facts required by the law. Others, such as the United States, consider that recognition is an act of sovereign discretion the exercise of which is not controlled by law. The net result is that there is confusion and dispute in the international community. The subject of recognition may be considered as one of the main defects of international law today.

ii. State Territory. Territory being a requisite of statehood and the area of the globe in which the state exercises its territorial sovereignty, international law is concerned with defining state territory, its manner of acquisition, disposal and loss. This territory of states includes its maritime areas, namely, the belt of sea adjacent to its coasts, and its airspace above the maritime and land territory. Today international law is also concerned with those parts of the bed and subsoil of the high seas lying beyond the territorial sea but at a depth at which their resources are exploitable. This is know as the 'continental shelf', which the coastal states have 'sovereign rights' to explore and exploit. There has been a considerable amount of new law established on these topics, both by custom and by law making, and notably by multilateral conventions under the initiative of the United Nations.

International law determines what rights states have in respect of the different types of territory, for example, home territory, colonies, protectorates, mandate and trust territories. The general rule is that states enjoy sovereignty over all persons and things within their territory, but there are a number of qualifications which the law has engrafted upon that basic principle. In the law relating to state territory the imprint of Roman private law rules about property is still quite marked.

iii. Jurisdiction. Jurisdiction is that degree of authority and control which international law confers upon a state over all persons and things within its territory, and its nationals, ships and aircraft outside its territory. By treaty a state may enjoy a certain jurisdiction in the territory of another state, being a derogation from the customary law situation. States also enjoy, by customary law, rights of protection over their nationals when present in the territory of foreign states. Complementary to the jurisdiction of states are the immunities enjoyed by such persons as diplomatic envoys, members of armed forces, crews of warships and members of international organisations, when present in the territory of a foreign state. Some of these immunities flow from customary law, for example, that of diplomatic envoys, while others flow from treaty, for example, visiting armed forces. Today the immunities and privileges of diplomatic envoys are governed by a general law-making Convention concluded at Vienna in 1961 and which came into force on April 24th, 1964.

Although a state has, by customary law, jurisdiction over aliens within its territory, the same law requires that certain minimum standards of good treatment be displayed to them. In default, and if local recourse has been exhausted, the state upon which the wronged alien depends may be entitled to assert its right of protection against that state failing to put right the wrong done. By customary law a state may treat its own nationals at discretion, but today treaty has made certain inroads upon that position.

Jurisdiction is also a matter of some importance on the high seas, an area of the world's surface which is not subject to the sovereignty of any state. So that order may be kept on the oceans, international law, as a general rule, limits the jurisdiction of states to their own ships, with the notable exception of piratical and slave trading ships, which are subject to the jurisdiction of all states.

iv. Individuals. International law being primarily, but not exclusively, concerned with states, individuals are not normally the holders of international law rights, although pirates and war criminals have been considered as the bearers of international law duties. Today the legal establishment of the idea of human rights, embodied in the Charter of the United Nations, has led to the direct conferment of rights upon individuals. These rights, carefully defined in the European Convention of Human Rights of 1951, may be asserted and enforced at the instance of the individual before international organs set up by that Convention. Such a situation derives from treaties. However, in the absence of such a treaty or convention the individual stands before international law as an object and not a repository of rights or duties. The United Kingdom is a party to the European Convention of Human Rights and has accepted the jurisdiction of the European Court of Human Rights and the individual right of petition to the European Commission of Human Rights, as from January 1966.

v. Treaties. Treaties are agreements between states creating legal rights and obligations between the parties. Customary law, still the central part of international law, in spite of the preponderance of treaties today, gives treaties their binding force. All states have the capacity to conclude treaties. International organisations, such as the United Nations, have a limited treaty-making competence, determined by their purposes and functions, as specified in their constituent instrument, itself a treaty. International law demands no particular form for a treaty, but requires that there shall be capacity and consent. The stress that international customary law has laid upon the binding nature of treaties has made the absence of any consideration or *quid pro quo* and the presence of duress irrelevant. Thus, treaties of peace concluded between the victors and the vanquished bind the parties. In spite of some dispute, the better opinion today is that treaties will not be upheld if they have an illegal purpose, for example, a treaty to commit aggression against a third State. Today such a treaty would be, apart from any other objection, a violation of the United Nations Charter. Further, by a provision of the Charter, obligations thereunder prevail over other treaty obligations inconsistent with the Charter.

International law is concerned with the manner in which treaties come into legal force, are discharged, breached and terminated. There is also a body of customary law rules relating to the interpretation of treaties and the circumstances in which the preliminary transaction leading to the treaty (*travaux préparatoires*) may be scrutinised to assist in its interpretation. It is recognised today that many treaties have more than a purely contractual effect limited to the parties to them. International organisations and institutions, such as the United Nations Organisation and the World Health Organisation, which abound and increase, are the creations of multilateral treaties. The codification and progressive development of international law is achieved in the same way, as can be seen in the four Geneva Conventions concerned with the law of the sea, established in 1958. Treaties may also be dispositive in their effects, for example, in a treaty providing for the cession of territory between the parties. At the moment there is being prepared by the International Law Commission, a subsidiary organ of the General Assembly of the United Nations, draft articles for a convention relating to the law of treaties.

vi. Settlement of Disputes. International law has generated a variety of devices for the pacific settlement of international disputes. The condemnation of the threat or use of aggressive force in Article 2 (4) of the United Nations Charter has subjected these devices to a strain that has exposed their weaknesses. The means of pacific settlement are those by which states agree between themselves the terms of settlement and those by which they are persuaded to accept a settlement arrived at by third parties. The former group includes such methods as good offices, mediation and conciliation. The latter embraces arbitration and judicial settlement. In arbitration the parties choose the umpire or arbitrator who acts only for the particular case referred to him. In judicial settlement the judge is a member of a standing court. Both methods presuppose the agreement of the contestant parties to submit their case for settlement. The International Court of Justice, created by the Charter of the United Nations, is competent to entertain cases between states only. Its powers of adjudication are limited to the extent to which the litigant states have accepted the Court's jurisdiction over the particular matter in dispute. Thus we do not have today an international court with a compulsory jurisdiction.

The International Court is also empowered to give advisory opinions on any legal question upon the request of the General Assembly or the Security Council. A valuable deposit of case law has been developed by the Court. States have, however, shown a considerable reserve in resorting to it. They have frequently accepted its jurisdiction, as they are entitled to under the 'Optional Clause' (Art. 36) of its Statute, with wide reservations and for strictly limited periods of time.

The Charter of the United Nations has thrown the primary responsibility for keeping the peace upon the Security Council. In the matter of the pacific settlement of disputes the Council may not dictate, but only recommend, measures and terms of settlement. It cannot direct, as it may when confronted with threats to the peace or aggression. Members are required to try out the existing methods of pacific settlement, mentioned above, before the Security Council attempts a solution, although the Council may investigate and recommend procedures at any stage, in disputes that look like disturbing the peace. The 'veto' voting provision has, however, seriously frustrated the role of the Council in achieving pacific settlement of international disputes. By this provision (Art. 27 (3)), the Security Council may not act in the face of a negative vote from any one of the five permanent members. This has led to some searching for improved procedures of settlement. The answer probably lies in the climate of opinion prevailing among states, reflected in their response to the requirements of the Charter of the United Nations. Members must fulfil their Charter obligations in good faith and settle their international disputes by peaceful means (Arts. 2 (2) and (3)). Improved machinery can achieve little in the absence of the will to reach a settlement and the good faith required to carry it out.

viii. The Regulation of Armed Force. Perhaps it is in this area of International Law that the swiftest and most impressive changes have been made. Within the space of less than fifty years states have given up their legal right to resort to war as an instrument of national policy. This right existed at the start of the First World War. At that time international law recognised the right of states to resort to war to assert rights denied, to revise treaties and to obtain redress for wrongs done, and for the furtherance of the policy of the moment. The Covenant of the League of Nations reduced the immediate resort to this right, but did not abolish the right, when pacific means, through the League's machinery, had failed. The Pact of Paris of 1928 required states to renounce war as an instrument of national policy, subject to the existing right of self-defence inhering in all states. This notable legal landmark has in its turn been overtaken, but not superseded, by Article 2 (4) of the Charter of the United Nations. Thereby Members must 'refrain in their international relations from the threat or use of force against the territorial integrity or political independence of any state'. This is probably the most extensive curtailment of the rights of states yet accepted. It now binds some 121 states. They have retained their inherent right of individual and collective self-defence. Also the Charter, in Chapter VII, created a scheme for the collective enforcement of the peace by the use of armed force provided by Members upon the call of the United Nations through the Security Council. Such use of force might either be directed, when there would be an obligation to respond, or be recommended, in which case the use of force by Members responding, without obligation, becomes a lawful use of force. It is this crucial part of the Charter that has been rendered inoperative by the use of the 'veto' in the Security Council. Improvised means of peacekeeping have been devised by the use of United Nations Forces, composed of national contingents under a United Nations Command, operating under Security Council authority where the veto did not operate, or of the General Assembly under the 'Uniting for Peace' Resolution adopted in December 1950. This latter device was adopted to meet the situation where the Council is frustrated from further action in keeping the peace by reason of the veto. Within limits, these devices have not been a failure, but the military roles of such United Nations Forces are restricted and the expense of operating such Forces, coupled with the refusal of certain members to contribute, has reduced the financial position of the United Nations so severely that a system of bond loans has had to be launched.

In former times a large part of international law, namely the law of war, controlled the manner in which wars were fought; for example, the means and weapons of combat, the treatment of the prisoners and wounded, and the occupation of territory. The new weaponry and military groupings of states, together with the increasing difficulty in keeping the civilian populations out of the combat—as indirect participants or as targets—has rendered much of the traditional law of war anachronistic and difficult to apply. Much of the law of combat is out of date, being governed by codifying Conventions of the late nineteenth century. Some attempt has been made to bring the law governing the treatment of war victims, prisoners, wounded and civilians up to date in the light of the harsh experiences of the Second World War. It cannot be denied, however, that the law of war is today in a confused condition and bears only a limited relationship to modern means of warfare and its all-embracing nature. Any attempt to distinguish between aggressor and victim in the application of the law of war has so far been resisted, although some discrimination against the aggressor may well be made in the non-acceptance of traditional belligerent rights in occupied territory, and the title to property seized, and the non-recognition of title to territory obtained in a successful but aggressive war.

In the area of the law of neutrality the Charter of the United Nations has made considerable, but as yet uncharted, inroads into the traditional law on this subject. In some situations the Charter leaves little room for the free play of the law of neutrality, but in the light of the frustration of the Security Council in its peacekeeping function there may be more play for neutrality law than was envisaged.

An Appraisal of International Law

It is valuable to try to adopt a balanced view of the role of international law in contemporary international affairs. Some sort of 'middle view' is needed. It is an error to expect this law to prevent all armed conflicts and to resolve all disputes. It is no less an error to dismiss it as a failure. Two considerations may help towards such a balanced view. First, when one considers the power of the states, the entities primarily bound by international law, it is surprising that so much has been achieved in the orderly conduct of interstate activities. Second, the public attention is normally directed to the major interstate clashes when armed force is threatened or used. There are other and substantial areas of international affairs, for example, in technical, economic and social co-operation, when international law works effectively and smoothly in the control of such affairs. It is sufficiently effective in those areas to attract little attention and to be accepted as the normal régime. This is a tribute to international law that is not dispelled by its failures in other and more dramatic spheres.

It is not so much the content of international law that is at fault although much of it needs modernising and to be given that degree of certainty which would encourage states to make increasing use of judicial settlement. The manner of its enforcement is weak, but that weakness is the reflection of the prevailing climate of opinion. What is needed is that which the law cannot itself produce, namely, an ever-increasing will among states to achieve peaceful settlement of their troubles, and a fuller measure of good faith with which to observe the terms of settlements and legal obligations, generally. In many spheres of international activity states have shown the will and the good faith required for successful co-operation. International law has its achievements and its failures. In the last resort its future lies in the hearts of men. International law is an essential part of our human destiny.

(B) PRIVATE INTERNATIONAL LAW

M. R. Chesterman

MOST PEOPLE ARE FAMILIAR with a number of stock situations which raise questions of Private International Law, but the precise scope and purpose of this subject and its distinctive characteristics are known to few outside the legal profession. It is common knowledge, for instance, that in certain circumstances a divorce granted in the United States will not carry any weight in England, but not many laymen know how this is to be explained, or even that the explanation forms part of a branch of law called Private International Law. Ignorance of these matters is not surprising, because Private International Law is a comparatively specialist topic. Yet, year by year, communication between nations increases and citizens of different countries have more and more dealings with each other, both on a personal level and in the course of their business; to the extent to which these trends continue, as they inevitably must, Private International Law will take on greater practical significance for ordinary people and their legal advisers. If England should become a member of the Common Market, one ventures to predict that solicitors and barristers throughout the country will be consulting almost daily their textbooks on Private International Law.

What, then, is the exact function of Private International Law? The short answer is that it solves certain vital preliminary issues in any legal dispute in which some 'international element' is present and one or more of the disputants is a private individual or a corporation. More precisely, when two or more nations or states, having different laws,[1] might each fairly claim that a dispute involving the legal rights of a private individual or a corporation should be governed by its law, Private International Law is used to sort the matter out. The dispute might, for example, relate to the ownership of French land forming part of the estate of a deceased Englishman, or to the extent to which a polygamous Muslim marriage should be recognised in England, or to the efficacy of an agreement between a New York company and a firm operating in Alabama, whereby goods are to be delivered from Portugal to Ceylon. Each of these situations has the 'international flavour' which calls for an application of the principles of Private International Law.

The most distinctive characteristic of Private International Law is the unusual process it adopts in resolving disputes of this sort. In theory, there are a number of alternative ways of handling them. Ideally, perhaps, such disputes would be sent off to an international tribunal to be dealt with according to a universally accepted system of international law. This does not in fact happen, because, as has been explained in the first part of this chapter, the large majority of existing international tribunals only hear cases brought by nations or international organisations, and, furthermore, no such system of international law exists for resolving private disputes, even though the term Private International Law may seem to imply something of the sort. In practice, therefore, these disputes are litigated in an ordinary court (such as the High Court of Justice in England) and are resolved according to the ordinary law of one or more of the countries with which the matter is in some way connected. This does not mean that the court in which proceedings have been instituted necessarily applies the law of its own country, for this would frequently be unjust or impracticable; instead, it chooses the law of whichever country seems appropriate for each major issue in the case. It is obvious that the Court must have at its disposal a set of legal rules by which to decide: (*a*) whether it should hear the case or refer it to some more appropriate forum in another country (this is the question of 'jurisdiction'); (*b*) what law it should apply for each aspect of the case if it does decide to hear it ('choice of law'); and (*c*) whether and to what extent any prior foreign judgment in the same case should be treated as conclusive ('recognition of foreign judgments'). The rules for deciding these three basic questions—jurisdiction, choice of law and recognition of foreign judgments—are the rules of Private International Law. It follows that in the vast majority of 'international' cases in the world today, rules devised according to this pattern are applied by the courts at the outset as a means of obtaining guidance towards their ultimate verdict.

It is to be stressed, however, that these rules provide 'guidance' only; they have in this respect been compared to an enquiry office at a railway station, which tells you which platform to go to in order to find your train but still leaves you relying on the train to take you to your destination. In other words, a hopeful litigant will not discover from Private International Law alone whether he is entitled to damages or a divorce, or any other remedy he may be seeking. At best, he will be told which particular local system of law—English, French, New York, etc.—is to determine his fate, and from this point onwards he must consult the rules there laid down, instead of Private International Law.

Furthermore, it is essential to realise that each country has its own set of Private International Law rules, which are administered as part of the ordinary law of the land. These rules differ considerably from country to country, and even, within the United States, from state to state. The absence of a universally accepted body of Private International Law principles can be explained on historical grounds; this branch of the law is an ancient one, having its beginnings in Roman times or even earlier, and in most countries the basic rules were formulated long before co-operation and communication among heads of state and their ministers had reached the stage at which international uniformity in a technical branch of the law could even be proposed as a feasible project, much less actually achieved. Theories of Private International Law (which have been particularly prolific on the Continent) did, of course, succeed in crossing the particular frontiers within which they were conceived, but no one theory ever achieved universal acceptance to the extent that every nation was prepared to implement it in practice. Thus present-day lawyers must cope with dissimilarities, often striking ones, between the existing systems of Private International Law. They can give rise to some peculiarly intractable problems, notably when a collision occurs between systems with radically different historical backgrounds: for example, a common-law system, of which English law is the prime example, and a civil-law system deriving from Roman law, such as the French. With a view to eradicating these problems, a Standing Conference on Private International Law was set up at The Hague at the end of the nineteenth century, and since 1951 it has worked continually at producing draft conventions for the unification of the rules of Private International Law of the member countries on specific topics. Unfortunately, it has not been very successful in obtaining acceptance of these conventions by the member nations. In the past fifteen years the United Kingdom has adopted three of them.

The major differences between Private International Law and Public International Law should now be apparent. Private International Law is part of a country's own law, designed to deal with the legal affairs of individuals and corporations when two or more countries become concerned with them. Public International Law is a genuinely international system of law, distinct from and (on one view, at least) overriding the internal laws of individual nations, and in general, it governs the legal relationships of the nations themselves and certain international organisations. Generally, these two branches of law operate independently of each other, but there are exceptional situations where they intersect, notably where the existence of sovereign or diplomatic immunities is in question.

The rest of this chapter will be devoted to a brief survey of the rules of English Private International Law, under the three principal headings of jurisdiction, choice of law and recognition of foreign judgments. Most of the law discussed is derived from decided cases; very little of it is statutory.

Jurisdiction

Naturally jurisdiction, the question whether the Court should hear the case before it, is the first point to be determined in the hearing of a case. If the Court decides that it lacks jurisdiction that is an end of the matter. According to English Private International Law, the prime test of jurisdiction is that the defendant must have been personally served with a writ of summons (which is in essence a command by Her Majesty to attend at her Courts of Justice) somewhere in England. Usually, nothing more than this need be shown. It is not wholly logical, nor even always just, that mere presence on English soil should be a sufficient basis of jurisdiction. It is conceivable that the defendant's sole reason for being in England is that he happens to be changing aeroplanes at London Airport in the course of a flight from Paris to New York; nevertheless, if the process-server catches him on the tarmac he will be subject to English jurisdiction unless he can claim one of the exceptions mentioned below.

An additional basis of jurisdiction is that the defendant agrees, in advance or after the proceedings are commenced, to let the case proceed in an English court. Also, the High Court of Justice may, at its discretion, assume jurisdiction in a number of specified instances, even though the defendant cannot be personally served in England. This discretion may be exercised, for example, where the case concerns a tort committed in England, or a contract made or broken in England. In such situations the Court must consider whether it is fair to the defendant to let the case proceed in England.

There are some important exceptions and qualifications to these general rules. In particular, an English court will refuse jurisdiction if the issue of title to foreign land is involved (this, it is said, is best left to the courts of the country in which the land is situated) or if a personal immunity to suit in England is proved by the defendant, or if an action has already been instituted elsewhere and the proceedings in England are chiefly designed to make things difficult for the defendant. Moreover, special rules are applied in matrimonial and family law cases. Here the most common requirement is not that the defendant happens to be present in England but that the plaintiff is 'domiciled' there. Domicile is a key concept in English Private International Law; it will crop up again in the course of this chapter. It can be broadly defined as the country or state where, according to the law, a person is to be treated as having his home. In normal circumstances a person's domicile (he can never be without one) will be that of his father at the time of his birth (a so-called 'domicile of origin') unless subsequently he has come to live in another country with an intention of remaining there permanently ('domicile of choice'). But there are qualifications, of which the most important are that a person below the age of 21 (called by the law an 'infant') generally has the same domicile as his father, and the domicile of a married woman is invariably that of her husband, even when she is separated from him.[2]

If the Court decides that it has jurisdiction according to these rules its next step is to decide which law to apply. This brings us to choice of law, which is the most important topic in Private International Law.

Choice of Law

The process of choosing which law to apply involves the use of a distinctive legal technique which at times must cope with very complex problems. The best way to explain this process in broad outline is to consider a specimen case.

Let us suppose that X, an Englishman, has established his permanent home in the state of New York, so that, in the eyes of English law, he has become 'domiciled' there. Without having made a will, he dies in New York, leaving a number of books and pieces of furniture which are situated in England. An English court is asked by one of X's surviving relatives to decide who is entitled to have the books and furniture. The Court concludes that it has jurisdiction, but then finds that New York law and English law differ on the legal issue at stake. As both 'countries'[3] seem to be involved in the matter, a choice has to be made between them.

On these facts, the Court would actually choose New York law. It would reach its conclusion by the following steps:

(*a*) This case poses a question of succession law, or, more specifically, of intestate succession to moveable property.

(*b*) English Private International Law prescribes that the appropriate law to determine a question of this type is the law of the deceased person's domicile at the date of his death.

(*c*) X was domiciled in New York when he died, and hence New York law should be applied.

Let us examine these three steps more closely. First, the Court, at stage (*a*), has identified the main issue in the case and described it in legal terms—'intestate succession to moveable property'. This is called 'classifying' the case. At its simplest, classification involves deciding to what general branch of the law (such as succession, contracts, matrimonial law, etc.) the case belongs. But usually, as has happened here, the nature of the case must be defined more specifically. The guiding principle is that the description ultimately arrived at for each major issue in the case must be such as to bring that issue under one, and one only, of the so-called 'choice of law' rules laid down in Private International Law. Classification, then, shows the way to a choice of law rule which the Court can apply to the facts of the case. In the above example the choice of law rule is proposition (*b*). What this proposition does, in effect, is to nominate the deceased man's domicile as the element in the case which is to be treated as decisive in 'locating' the case for legal purposes. It says that because X was domiciled in New York at the time of his death the issue of inheritance of his moveable property should be taken to be 'situated' in New York also, and should therefore be subject to New York law.

Domicile here is said to be the 'connecting factor'. All choice of law rules operate through connecting factors, which frequently vary from rule to rule. For example, had the property owned by X been English land, instead of books and furniture in England, a different choice of law rule, covering intestate succession to *immoveable* property, would have been applicable. It would have named the situation of the land as the connecting factor, and consequently English law, not New York law, would have been selected by the Court.

This, briefly, is the procedure adopted by an English court when confronted by a question of choice of law; it now remains to consider the substance of the choice of law rules themselves. They are often detailed and technical, but the broad effect of the more important ones can be concisely summarised. Most matters of matrimonial law, family law, personal status and succession are assigned to the law of the domicile of one of the parties involved. Litigation arising out of a contract is governed primarily by the so-called 'proper law' of the contract, that is to say, the system of law with which the contract is found to be most closely connected; subject to certain recognised limitations, the parties to the contract may themselves stipulate what law this is to be. In tort cases a peculiar 'double rule' operates, whereby the Court consults both English law and the law of the place where the alleged tort was committed. In cases involving land the *lex situs*, which means the law of the country where the land is situated, is almost invariably used. However, where the subject matter of the dispute is moveable property, there are a number of possible connecting factors: the *situs* of the property, the domicile of its owner, the place where the property was last sold or the 'proper law' of the sale. Procedural matters are always governed by the law of the Court in which the case is being tried (the *lex fori*).

These rules embody the attempt of English law to ensure that the system of law which is naturally appropriate to the case should be applied to it. In their development a number of factors have had to be taken into account, factors such as fairness to both parties, the requirement that the decision should be readily enforceable, the interests of the communities in which the parties habitually reside and, not least, the expectations and intentions of the parties themselves. In this respect, Private International Law, as much as any other branch of the law, has its roots in considerations of justice and social policy.

Indeed, there are certain special cases where the demands of policy in this field are so great that established choice of law rules are overridden. Foreign revenue laws and penal laws, for instance, will not be directly enforced in this country. Moreover, a more general principle of 'public policy' exists, whereby application of the foreign law indicated by normal choice of law rules may be withheld to prevent infringement of fundamental moral or legal precepts or distinctive national policies. The scope of the 'public policy' doctrine is not clear, and it has cropped up in all sorts of diverse contexts, but fortunately it has generally been reserved for situations where the issues at stake are too fundamental to be solved by the mechanical application of technical rules. In other words, it is treated as a rule of last resort, to be used sparingly and only after very careful consideration by the Court.

Recognition and Enforcement of Foreign Judgments

Compared with choice of law, this is a subsidiary topic only. The question of recognition arises when a successful plaintiff in a foreign action seeks to enforce his judgment in England, or when the defendant in an English action pleads that the matter in issue has already been settled by a binding foreign judgment.

In this field the all-important criterion is jurisdiction; if the foreign court had jurisdiction according to English rules its judgment is recognised in England. By way of example, the recognition of a foreign divorce decree depends primarily, and almost solely, on whether the plaintiff was domiciled in the foreign country at the time when proceedings were commenced, because this is the major test of jurisdiction in divorce cases in England. In a case[4] in 1870 a foreign court, having sufficient qualifications in terms of jurisdiction, had applied English law to the facts of the case, but had seriously misinterpreted the relevant rule of English law; nevertheless, its judgment was recognised by an English court. Here it seems that excessive importance was attached to jurisdiction. However, there are some situations where recognition is refused even though the foreign court is shown to have jurisdiction. Briefly, these are where the foreign judgment was obtained through fraud, or without both sides having an opportunity to present their cases adequately, or where it seeks to enforce a foreign penal or revenue law or contravenes English 'public policy'. In addition, it was said in a recent case[5] in the Court of Appeal that any foreign judgment which is 'substantially unjust' may be refused recognition on that ground alone, but the limits of this principle have not yet been determined. Clearly, it should not be pressed too far, because *prima facie* the successful party should be entitled to assume that any judgment in his favour, wherever delivered, should be enforceable anywhere else in the world, and it is only in exceptional circumstances that his expectations should be disappointed.

By way of conclusion, it is appropriate to draw attention

to an aspect of Private International Law which has already been mentioned in passing: namely, the remarkable way in which it combines diverse matters of intense theoretical and practical significance. For centuries it has been the subject of widespread discussion and argument among jurists, and abstract theories of all kinds have been put forward to explain the subject in general terms and to provide a framework from which specific principles might be derived. None of these theories has been wholly convincing, yet almost all have been stimulating and have contributed to the development of the subject. At the same time, Private International Law must be used by the practitioner at all levels of practice. No case is too small or too large to be within its reach, and no area of the law is so remote that a dispute governed by it may not also pose problems of Private International Law. Hence, Private International Law is a subject of prime importance for both academic lawyers and legal practitioners. Moreover, its importance must inevitably increase as the communities of the world come steadily into closer contact with each other.

Suggested Reading

A. PUBLIC INTERNATIONAL LAW

J. L. BRIERLY, *The Law of Nations*, Clarendon Press.

L. OPPENHEIM, *International Law*, 2 vols., Vol. I, *Peace*, Vol. II, *Disputes, War and Neutrality*, Longmans, Green.

D. P. O'CONNELL, *International Law*, 2 vols., Stevens.

J. G. STARK, *An Introduction to International Law*, Butterworths.

PHILIP C. JESSUP, *A Modern Law of Nations*, Macmillan: New York.

THE CHARTER OF THE UNITED NATIONS AND THE STATUTE OF THE INTERNATIONAL COURT OF JUSTICE, U.N. Office of Public Information, H.M.S.O.

B. PRIVATE INTERNATIONAL LAW

R. H. GRAVESON, *The Conflict of Laws*, Sweet & Maxwell.

G. C. CHESHIRE, *Private International Law*, Oxford University Press.

F. HARRISON, *On Jurisprudence and the Conflict of Laws*, Ch. IV–V, Oxford University Press.

NOTES

[1] The essential point is that the systems of law which might conceivably govern the dispute have different content and so are notionally in conflict with one another; this is the reason why Private International Law is often called Conflict of Laws. It also explains why purely interstate transactions within federations whose member states have different laws (such as the United States and Australia) are regarded by Private International Law as 'international'.

[2] These two principles can obviously come into conflict; when they do, the latter prevails, which means that a wife under twenty-one takes her husband's domicile, not her father's.

[3] As was pointed out earlier, the State of New York is a 'country' for Private International Law purposes, because it has its own system of law.

[4] *Godard* v. *Gray* (1870) L.R. 6 Q.B. 139.

[5] *Gray* v. *Formosa* (1963) P. 259.

II

Law as a Career

D. B. Parker

A SURPRISINGLY LARGE number of people seem to be unaware that the legal profession in England and Wales is divided into two branches—the Bar and the Solicitors' Branch. And many of those who know of the distinction appear to have a curious and unrealistic impression of the kind of work which each of them does. The popular image of the profession often falls into one or other of two extremes. One (derived from the cinema and television) is that a barrister is primarily concerned with criminal cases in Court—an English variant of Perry Mason; the other is that a solicitor spends most of his time in perusing ancient documents and other equally boring occupations. For both branches it is often believed that huge tomes on law have to be learned by heart. The vestige of truth that lies in all these propositions is particularly slight. The purpose of this chapter is to consider briefly the training demanded of a lawyer and his prospects in practice and elsewhere.

Initial Training

A boy or girl leaving school will usually wish to go to a university and take a degree. This is not an essential preliminary to becoming a barrister or solicitor, and may delay professional qualification. But the intellectual and social experience of university life is invariably thought desirable for a prospective lawyer—except perhaps by a few of those who have never attended a university. In fact, an increasing number of newly qualified solicitors and barristers domiciled in this country are university graduates. What a prospective lawyer should read at the university is a question on which opinions are divided. The most obvious course is to take a law degree, but some people believe that he should read something else, for example, classics or history, or a mixture of subjects, so to get what is thought to be a wider cultural background. The 'mixed' degree is a striking feature of the newly established universities. However, a university course in law pure and simple does provide certain clear advantages. There is the practical one that if a student takes a law degree he may obtain exemption from part of the examinations for both branches of the profession and, for the intending solicitor, his period of articles will be shorter. But more generally, a university law course carries the positive advantage of providing a rigorous training in a recognised academic discipline.

Most English universities provide courses in law, and these stretch over a three-year period. They are not at all identical, but essentially the object of them all is to provide a grounding in the general principles of the law in its major aspects. Students reading law at university can generally choose between an LL.B. (Bachelor of Laws) and a B.A. (Law) degree. The B.A. (Law) degree has not yet been fully worked out, and it may vary in different institutions. It is not yet known what exemptions will apply to it. In all cases the Faculties of Law at the universities should be consulted by the intending student. Curricula today are going through a process of modernisation. The emphasis is shifting from subjects like Roman Law and Legal History to subjects with more modern relevance like Company Law, Family Law and Income Tax Law, and this seems a step which is long overdue. But whatever legal subjects a man may have read at the university, he will not be fitted for practice. A three-year law course for people with no previous background in law cannot achieve that, nor is that its purpose. Its purpose is to examine not only some of the detailed rules of law but also the reasons for those rules and their relationship to other aspects of society. It is designed to be academic. Competence in legal practice depends on practical experience and aptitude.

The pressure on university places is nowadays so acute that some will not succeed in obtaining admission. In this event they may choose, if otherwise qualified, to start training immediately to be a barrister or solicitor. They may still be able to take an external degree at London University, and courses for this are provided in technical colleges and Colleges of Further Education throughout the country. Some ambitious individuals may try to combine such a course with their practical training, but this often proves an onerous task and difficult to sustain.

Once a student has successfully taken his degree (or before) he may decide to enter practice. He will then have to make up his mind whether he wishes to practise as a barrister or as a solicitor. One of the peculiarities of the English system is that the Bar and the solicitors' branch are separate. It is not possible to be a barrister and a solicitor at the same time. The legal profession in most other countries in the world (including the United States and most of the Commonwealth) is fused: there is only one class of lawyer who is qualified—if not always competent—to do the work of both a barrister and solicitor here. Voices have been raised in recent years in favour of uniting the two branches in this country. The argument is that a united profession is less expensive and more convenient. The counter-argument is that the existence of a separate Bar makes for a high standard of advocacy and also ensures detachment and integrity, because the barrister can only receive his instructions through a solicitor, and is, therefore, not so bound up with the interests of the lay client as a solicitor must inevitably be. The 'fusionists' have not as yet gained general support in the profession, and consequently a would-be lawyer has to make his choice at a very early stage. He may, of course, feel later that he has chosen wrongly and that the other branch of the profession would suit him better. He is entitled in such a case to make the change, but under present regulations will have to take the examinations required by the other branch, even though he has already passed the examinations for the one he first selected. The reasons are that the examinations and training for the two branches are different, as are the examining bodies, the Council of Legal Education for the Bar, and the Law Society for the solicitors' branch. There is a strong case for providing a common legal examination for both branches, even if it is thought that the time has not yet arrived for a fusion of the profession itself.

The Bar

This is dealt with first because it is traditionally the senior of the two branches of the profession. The Bar is also hedged around with many customs and formalities. Many of these no doubt have a useful purpose, but they are only imperfectly understood by the layman, and require a fairly detailed explanation.

The first step for an aspiring barrister is to be admitted as a student to one of the four Inns of Court, and this is necessary whether he has taken a university degree or not. The Inns are Lincoln's Inn, the Inner Temple, the Middle Temple and Gray's Inn. The academic standard for admission is not especially high. Passes in five subjects in the G.C.E., including two at advanced level, or in four subjects, including three at advanced level, are the minimum required.

The Inns of Court are a somewhat surprising legacy from the Middle Ages, and most laymen are mystified by them. They are independent entities with the legal status of unincorporated associations. Originally founded as long ago as the fourteenth century, their original purpose was to provide legal instruction to prospective lawyers. But this function is now performed by the Council of Legal Education on behalf of all the Inns. They now provide a 'home' for their members, who can, whether students or barristers, lunch and dine together at reasonable cost and in pleasant surroundings.

Joining an Inn is not, of course, enough in itself. Apart from passing the usual examinations, students are bound, before being called to the Bar (as admission to this branch of the profession is described), to eat a number of dinners in their Inn. The technical expression for this is 'keeping term in person'. There are four dining terms each year of twenty-three days' duration in each term, and a student must generally dine in the Hall of his Inn on three separate days in each term over a period of three years. This curious system is highly formal, and its preservation has met with some criticism in recent years on the ground that it serves no useful purpose. However, many people are convinced of the value dinners (together with moots, debates and other social activities) have in fostering a corporate spirit in early days at the Bar which endures over the years. This is perhaps buttressed by the fact that each of the Inns has itself until very recently been responsible for the discipline of the barristers and students who are its members. The Inn acts in all matters through its governing body, the Masters of the Bench, or Benchers as they are often called, who sit in Hall apart from the others. They are self-electing and are composed of the judiciary and other men of standing at the Bar.

A Senate of the four Inns of Court has now been established, and the Inns and the Bar Council (the representative body of the practising Bar) are represented on it. It deals with important matters affecting the profession generally, in particular education and discipline, which until recently have been the responsibility of each of the Inns and on which common action was possible only if unanimity could be achieved. This body seems to go a long way to providing more consistency in the running of this branch of the profession. It is only surprising that it has taken so long to come to fruition.

Although each Inn is autonomous and has its own traditions and history, there is a basic uniformity about them. This means from a practical standpoint that a prospective barrister will not be prejudiced by joining one Inn rather than another. The only Inn which may be said to have a traditional preserve in a given area of practice is Lincoln's Inn. This is regarded as the home of the Chancery Bar, which carries on business in the Inn itself. There are obvious advantages to a man who definitely intends to become a Chancery practitioner in joining Lincoln's Inn, because his chambers will be only a few yards from Hall and many of his colleagues on the Chancery side will also be members. But this is not essential. In any case, a student, when first joining an Inn, will not usually be sure of the work he would like to do at the Bar and he will tend to join the Inn with which he may have family connections or of which his friends are members.

The fees for membership of an Inn are fairly low, bearing in mind that they confer, if nothing else, lifetime membership of what can be regarded as a club. Payments for admission as a student and for call to the Bar are in the region of £180.

The next step for a student is to pass the Bar examinations. These are divided into two Parts: Part I and the Final. A law graduate of a University who has passed at a satisfactory standard should obtain exemption from the whole or part of Part I. Those without a law degree must face it. But to make life relatively easy, it could formerly be attempted subject by subject: now it is divided into two parts. The Bar Final is different: it is obligatory for all and must be passed as a whole. This is designed to be a practical examination, but it has many similarities to a university examination in law, and candidates may have dealt with most, if not all, of the subjects at the University. The basic difference is that much more has to be done in less time, and it requires a more comprehensive, if less profound, knowledge of legal subjects. The failure rate in the Final in recent years has been very high, at times reaching 70 per cent; but this is largely accounted for by the special circumstance that the vast majority of candidates are overseas students with limited experience of English examinations. A law graduate should have little difficulty in passing the examination after one year's intensive study from graduation. Because of the high failure rates, the Council of Legal Education has stipulated that a candidate cannot attempt the examination more than four times.

Lectures and tutorials are provided by the Council of

Legal Education, and also by the College of Law (the solicitors' academy). In addition, scholarships and prizes are awarded by each of the Inns of Court to persons intending to practise at the Bar. A few of these can be worth as much as £400 a year for a period of three to four years. Many of them are not awarded entirely upon performance in the Bar examinations. Other factors may be taken into account, and the view has been expressed (with perhaps rather less justification recently) that preference is unduly exercised in favour of those with a public school and Oxford or Cambridge background. The scholarships are designed to assist young men and women during the first penurious years at the Bar.

After successfully passing the Bar examinations, the aspiring barrister will now be about twenty-two or twenty-three years old. He will not, as yet, have earned any money, but he is still not equipped to practise. He may have taken a university law degree and passed the Bar Final and been called to the Bar. But so far his experience may have been entirely academic. He may never have been inside a court. Some practical training is therefore essential. This is provided at the Bar through the medium of a 'pupilage'. And to reinforce the need for practical training it is now stipulated that a barrister cannot accept any work at the Bar unless he has first served a pupilage for at least six months.

A pupilage requires that a man becomes a pupil to a junior barrister. The term 'junior' is perhaps misleading. It does not mean that the barrister is young. He may be in his thirties, but he may also be in his sixties. A junior is simply a practising member of the Bar who is not Queen's Counsel, or, in the language of the profession, has not taken silk.

The question now is, how does a newly-called barrister become a pupil? Surprisingly, although the Inns are making a greater effort to act as a kind of clearing house, selection of a pupil-master is still something of a lottery. A man with genuine legal connections may get good advice, but people without these advantages are likely to go to someone of whom they will know only through uninstructed hearsay.

He may turn out to be someone with too little practice to give much effective guidance, or with a practice so specialised and complex as to be above the head of a beginner, or he may be far too busy to be bothered with his pupil. Or he may turn out to be entirely suitable. It seems unfortunate that a rather more rational (and centrally superintended) system has not been devised. The only advice that can be proffered is that one should try to find a place with a junior of sound practice in both chambers and the courts and who also has sufficient time to give some instruction. However, despite all the possible disadvantages a pupilage is admittedly cheap. For over a hundred years the fee has remained static at 100 guineas for twelve months.

It is at this stage that the barrister must make up his mind what he wants to do. His choice will essentially lie between the common-law Bar and the Chancery Bar. This is putting it at its most simple, because the common-law Bar is itself divided into a number of specialisations. In London it is concentrated in the area south of Fleet Street known as the Temple. The bulk of the work is criminal, divorce and general civil matters (for example, factory and road accidents) and most chambers in the Temple (and the provinces) hold themselves ready to do all of this. But there are some chambers wholly based in London which, for example, will only do crime or divorce work. There are also others whose speciality is rather more exotic. They may be purely concerned with commercial law, or patents and copyright, or revenue law, or town and country planning. But most people at the common-law Bar today are general practitioners in the sense that their work will involve crime, divorce and unspecialised civil work, and will require them to act in both an advisory capacity and as advocates in the courts.

The other Bar is the Chancery Bar, and its home is in Lincoln's Inn, north of Fleet Street. There is little scope for a Chancery practitioner in the provinces, except in Manchester and Liverpool, where an active Chancery Court (the Court of the County Palatine of Lancaster) operates. Compared with the Temple, the Chancery Bar is very small.

Whereas there are about 160 sets of chambers in the Temple, there are only about 30 in Lincoln's Inn. The Chancery Bar is primarily concerned with trusts, property, company law and the administration of estates, though tax and estate duty work is of increasing importance. There is less advocacy to be done here than elsewhere. It requires a different temperament, and is more exacting intellectually than the general common-law Bar, but perhaps provides for a more placid existence.

But a man may not want to practise in London. He may prefer the provinces. The larger cities, such as Birmingham, Leeds and Manchester, maintain large local Bars, mostly general common law, with an emphasis on crime, divorce and industrial accidents. He may be well advised to become a pupil in such a centre, particularly if he has a local background there.

He will also, if intending to practise at the general common-law Bar, have to join a circuit. The country is divided up into various parts—seven in all—known by this title. If he hopes, for example, to work primarily in Lancashire he will join the Northern Circuit, if in Yorkshire the North-Eastern Circuit. Until recently the circuit system was highly restrictive, and although a member of one circuit could appear at Assizes or Quarter Sessions in another, a special circuit fee had to be paid. This naturally discouraged solicitors from instructing outsiders to do work in a foreign circuit. The rule has now been abolished. Nevertheless, it is still essential to join a circuit, because local solicitors will continue to instruct barristers who are known to them, and these will tend to be members of the circuit in their own territory. A circuit mess held periodically throughout the year provides a useful social meeting-place.

On the termination of pupilage he will then have to find a seat in chambers, because only barristers with recognised chambers are entitled to practise. This may be easier said than done. There is no assurance that he will be able to stay on in the chambers where he was a pupil. It will also be obvious that it is more difficult to enter chambers with a high reputation and a considerable turnover of work than others. A man will try to get into the best chambers because, assuming he has the necessary aptitude, his prospects will naturally be more favourable. If the chambers are busy it is more likely that some work will trickle down to him reasonably quickly, or he will have the opportunity of 'devilling', that is, working anonymously for another barrister and being paid half the fee. There may also be opportunities of inheriting work when a member of the chambers becomes a judge, or retires, or dies. But there is no certainty that work will devolve in this way, because solicitors may choose to send it out of chambers. It must always be remembered that a barrister can only receive instructions in a case from a solicitor, and a solicitor is in no way bound to send his work to any one barrister rather than another.

The problem of how barristers' chambers operate is one which has often puzzled the writers of detective fiction. The essence of a barrister's status is that he is self-employed. He contributes to rent for chambers and general office expenses and also, where demanded, the clerk's retainer. He is associated with other members of chambers and may see them every day, but he works for himself. He is not engaged on a salary and has no assurance that he will earn a penny. The general office management of the chambers for all its members, as well as the negotiation of their fees, is in the hands of the clerk of chambers. Every set of chambers must have a clerk for this purpose. Because it is the clerk who deals with solicitors, he can be helpful, especially in general common-law work, in finding work for a newly called barrister. He will usually take a percentage, perhaps 5 to 10% of the fees earned by the members of chambers, and in addition he may claim a retainer of about a £1 a week.

A young barrister who has recently been offered a seat in chambers must reckon on paying out at least £5–£6 a week in expenses of one form or another. He will usually pay more as his work increases. He may also have to pay circuit fees, and if he travels around the country, his travelling and hotel expenses. His chambers expenses will be slightly higher in London than in the provinces.

Prospects at the Bar

One occasionally reads in the newspapers of vast sums said to be earned by fashionable barristers, sometimes up to £30,000 a year. This is usually journalistic guesswork and, in any case, it is a grievous error to imagine that a barrister has a natural expectation of earning an income of this magnitude. Figures are difficult to come by, but one's impression is that the vast majority of practitioners are earning no more and no less than members of other professions. An established man of consistently sound practice will probably earn something in the region of £4,000 to £5,000 a year. Some will earn more, sometimes considerably more, and some will earn appreciably less.

The Bar in recent years has become relatively more prosperous. This has been particularly true of criminal work, because of the increase in crime and the availability of legal aid (provided by the State for payment of fees) to accused persons of limited means. It is, and always has been, easier to make a start in certain classes of work than in others. Given aptitude, it has always been perhaps easiest of all at the criminal Bar, not only because there has always been a great deal of crime but also because the clients are often poor. It is perhaps slowest of all at the Chancery Bar, where the subject-matter is technical and large sums of money are often at stake: solicitors are reluctant to entrust this kind of work to a callow youth. Putting it generally, it may also be quicker to make a start in the provinces than in London, though the greatest financial rewards—the so-called 'glittering prizes'—are for the London man. Perhaps the specialisation which provides the highest rewards of all to an effective practitioner is the Revenue Bar. But to achieve success in this highly specialised branch of the profession requires a very high degree of experience and 'know-how'.

With reasonable luck and ability a barrister should be able to make a very reasonable living. But it should never be forgotten that he lacks security. He is always dependent on work being sent to him by a solicitor. Consistent success also requires continuing physical fitness. Opportunities for delegation (other than occasional devilling) do not exist. And because everything depends on the barrister personally, he has nothing to sell when he retires.

The Bar is itself divided into two parts: the junior Bar and Queen's Counsel. The title 'Q.C.' has always fired the public imagination. In order to become a Q.C. a junior must 'apply for silk' to the Lord Chancellor—'silk', because a Q.C. wears a silk gown in court. It is granted to persons of established reputation at the Junior Bar. They may, among other reasons, feel that they are so overworked as juniors that a period as a silk with less work but higher fees would be attractive. But there are dangers in this. A Q.C. can only appear in court supported by a junior, and it follows that he tends to be instructed by solicitors only in cases of some significance, because two sets of fees have to be paid. Some Q.C.'s may therefore have a very lean time indeed. This may be alleviated to some extent by a recent ruling of the Bar Council relaxing the 'two-thirds rule'. This rule formerly made it imperative in most cases for a junior to be paid at least two-thirds of the fee demanded by his leader (as the Q.C. is also often called), even though the junior might do very little in actual conduct of the case. The junior's fee is now to be the subject of independent negotiation untrammelled by the rule. There is a further difficulty facing a Q.C. This is that he takes no part in the formulations of pleadings, that is, the written statement of the case to be put before the Court; this is within the exclusive province of the junior. The Q.C. is therefore automatically deprived of a source of income. In fact, he will be engaged primarily as an advocate, although he will also do a fair amount of advisory work, particularly at the Chancery Bar.

Yet another peculiarity may bear rather harshly on the provincial practitioner. He is entitled to take silk, but he has to move his chambers to London. And this may possibly mean that he will lose his local influence, unless he joins London chambers with a strong provincial connection.

Taking silk is often a preliminary to further 'prizes'. The judiciary is recruited entirely from the Bar—a system which has been attacked in recent years as 'unfair to solicitors'. Naturally membership of the High Court, with an automatic knighthood and tremendous prestige and with future expectations of a place in the Court of Appeal and the House of Lords, is the ambition of those who seek judicial preferment. The salaries for the High Court and Court of Appeal are £10,000 a year and pensionable: for the House of Lords, £11,250. Of course, only a tiny proportion of practising barristers can expect to become High Court Judges. But there are other opportunities, notably as a County Court Judge, or as Stipendiary Magistrate, with pensionable salaries of up to £5,000 a year. Other possibilities exist for practitioners of sufficient standing in the criminal courts as Recorder or Chairman of Quarter Sessions, which provide a regular source of income and can also be combined with practice at the Bar. There are other consolation prizes, if they can be so called, such as posts as Official Referees, Bankruptcy Registrars, Registrars of Companies, Masters of the Queen's Bench Division and Clerks of Assizes, all of which command a reasonable and secure income. For the established barrister–politician preferment to Attorney-General or Solicitor-General is possible, or at the pinnacle of the profession, as Lord Chancellor.

Solicitors

Despite all its uncertainties and peculiarities, there is no doubt that the Bar has appealed in the past, and possibly will continue to appeal in its present form to a few people every year. But whereas there are about 2,000 practising barristers, there are over 20,000 solicitors in practice. And the vast majority of those who intend to practise law will join the solicitors' branch. It has been seen that the Bar has its own rather novel traditions, which are difficult for an outsider to understand; the solicitors' branch is more straightforward and requires rather less explanation.

It is the solicitor with whom the general public comes into contact, for by one of the conventions governing life at the Bar, the lay client can instruct a barrister only through a solicitor. He therefore lives in a less-rarefied world. It may be less glamorous in the public imagination, but it is also less uncertain and perhaps less exacting. Solicitors are entitled to, and often do, enter into partnership with one another, whereas a barrister is dependent entirely on his own efforts. Accordingly, there is a genuine possibility of delegation not only to a partner but also to other employees of the firm. Delegation in this form is not possible at the Bar. Furthermore, a solicitor's practice, unlike a barrister's, can be disposed of on retirement or death, and this can be of considerable value.

What work does a solicitor do, and how does he fit into the legal profession in this country? A large proportion of the public will have had dealings of one sort or another with a solicitor, and the type of work he does is (to the initiated) reasonably well known. For example, if you buy a house it is the solicitor who drafts the contract for sale, investigates the title to the property and draws the conveyance. Conveyancing work of this kind is usually one of the staples of a solicitor's practice. It is also an aspect of practice which has attracted a good deal of adverse criticism lately. In any conveyancing job a solicitor is statutorily entitled to a fee based on the value of the land. This is on a sliding scale and varies in accordance with value. For example, for a house worth £4,000 he will take a fee of approximately £60 if the property is unregistered, or about £40 if it is registered. In some, though relatively few, parts of the country the title is compulsorily registrable at the Land Registry. If it is, the State guarantees the title, and if anything goes wrong provides compensation. It can be argued that fees of this size are far too high in cases where the title is guaranteed in this way. As to un-registered land, there are two sides to the argument. On the one hand, the title in question may be so well known in the area as to render the investigation almost entirely routine. On the other hand, it may be novel and highly complex and take up so much time as to make the fee unrealistically low. With the extension of compulsory land registration throughout the country, a cheaper system—possibly organised by the Land Registry itself—should perhaps be instituted to conduct an increasingly mechanical exercise.

Even if this one day happens, there is still a great deal of work for the solicitor to do. This will include the drafting of wills and the probate of wills on a testator's death. He also frequently acts as executor and administrator. He will be concerned with the formation of companies and the many legal problems that arise from time to time during the company's existence. He will be expected to advise on income-tax and estate-duty liability. He will be approached first on matters involving legal proceedings. He will be expected to give his views, although these may later be submitted to a barrister for further consideration, on whether a husband or wife has sufficient grounds for a divorce and also on all the volatile problems of custody of children and financial settlements. He will give his initial opinion on questions involving civil liability, as in road and factory accidents. A person accused in criminal proceedings will also come to a solicitor for guidance in the early stages of the case. These are merely examples. There is really no limit in this increasingly complex world to the matters on which a lay client may seek a solicitor's advice. However, it must not be thought from this brief account that a solicitor is necessarily 'desk-bound'. He has the opportunity, which relatively few take except in the most routine of cases, to engage in advocacy in certain courts. He has a right of audience in the Magistrates' Courts and in the County Court. In other courts it is only the barrister who has the right to be heard, although it has recently been recommended that the County Court should have jurisdiction to deal with divorce proceedings. This would enable solicitors to conduct them and would, incidentally, if it is accepted, cut the cost of obtaining a divorce. He will, in any case, have the job of preparing a case for a barrister ('a case for Counsel' as it is called) and will interview the witnesses and take statements from them. He will also from time to time instruct Counsel to give an opinion in a case where he thinks an expert view is necessary and will also usually instruct him to settle the pleadings for legal proceedings.

193

The majority of solicitors will deal with rich and poor alike and have to be ready to advise them on a host of problems. However, as one might expect, a member of one of the larger firms will tend to specialise in one or two branches of the law. Some (though very few) firms will deal with given classes of work only: for example, some, particularly in the City of London, refuse to touch crime or divorce. But to anyone who wants it there is the opportunity of doing a wide variety of work and meeting a large cross-section of the public, and trying to help them. And in any case, however specialised the solicitor may become, he is, unlike a barrister, brought directly into contact with the lay public. This may be more satisfying to some people than the necessary aloofness of the Bar.

How does someone become a solicitor? Again, like a prospective barrister, he must satisfy certain examination requirements. The minimum standard for enrolment as a student with the Law Society is a pass in five subjects in the G.C.E., including two subjects passed at A level, or passes in four subjects, including three at A level. One of these subjects must be English. A British or Irish university degree is also accepted in lieu. He will also have to attend for interview to decide if he is suitable for the moment to enrol as a student (he may be thought to be too immature). After passing over these hurdles, he must next take account of two things, first, articles of clerkship, and secondly, the Law Society's Qualifying Examination. It is essential for all prospective solicitors to serve under articles of clerkship with a practising solicitor. This amounts to an apprenticeship: the object is to teach an articled clerk how to become a solicitor through the medium of practical experience. But the duration of articles may vary quite considerably. It is here that a university degree will have material advantages. If the articled clerk has not taken a degree he must serve under articles for five years and must also attend a course of legal instruction at the College of Law in London or at certain provincial centres before attempting Part I of the Qualifying Examination. Or, alternatively, he can attend such a course and pass Part I before entry into articles. In this case the period of articles will be four years. The course of instruction in each case will last for about eight months.

For the graduate the position is different. If he has taken a *law* degree he becomes entitled to exemption from the whole or almost the whole of Part I, because he will have taken the whole or most of the subjects at the University. He has, like everybody else, to pass Part II of the Law Qualifying Examination, but he is entitled, if wholly exempt from Part I, to take Part II before entering into articles. If he does this, assuming he passed in not less than three heads of Part II, his period of articles will be reduced to two years. An alternative presents itself: he can take Part II during articles. In this case his period of articles will be for two and a half years. There are also concessions for graduates in other subjects than law. They will usually have to take Part I. They can do this before entry into articles, and, if so, the articles will last for two and a half years; or they can take it during articles, in which case they will last for three years. The period of articles can, therefore, range, depending on a man's qualifications, from two to five years.

Part I of the Qualifying Examination is reasonably straightforward, like Part I of the Bar Examination. It is Part II, again like the Bar Final, which is the gateway to the profession. It is an exacting examination, perhaps more testing than the Bar. It is, in so far as a written examination can be, a more practical exercise. The failure rate—about 30 per cent—is high, bearing in mind that there are few overseas students. For both Part I and Part II, a candidate who has first passed in three papers (out of a total of six and seven respectively) can take the rest of the papers in that part one by one. There is (unlike the Bar) no limit to the number of times either part of the examination can be attempted. A man will usually expect to spend at least six months' intensive and uninterrupted study for Part II of the Qualifying Examination.

The fees payable are £20 for enrolment as a student with the Law Society and a fee of three guineas per examination paper. The cost of tuition for each part of the examination is about £70.

It is the articles of clerkship which provide the practical backbone to a future solicitor's training. It has been seen that the minimum period for law graduates is two years. But it is stipulated that—for them and everybody—an uninterrupted period of two years under articles *must* be served. And during that period there is no time off to pursue any other activity.

How does one become articled and what does it involve? Naturally, it is necessary to find a solicitor who is willing to take one as an articled clerk. Family connections with the profession are perhaps the most useful of all. But only a few have genuine contacts; the others have to take advice. This may be forthcoming from the universities or local law societies, or from the Law Society itself. The most important point always to bear in mind is that one should try to obtain as wide a practical experience as possible, not just in one branch of the law but in as many as are available—to have some experience of commercial, conveyancing, civil, criminal and divorce work if this is possible. It is the principal's duty personally, or through his firm, to provide this kind of comprehensive background. It would be an ideal world if articles were always successful in this ambitious aim. No doubt their quality varies considerably with the quality of the principal and his firm. Moreover, a successful solicitor is often extremely busy and may have little time to give instruction. Indeed, it is unfortunate—but not to be marvelled at—that some articled clerks feel themselves to be regarded either as unmitigated nuisances or as a form of cheap labour. Nevertheless, whatever complaints have been voiced at its practical working in some cases, it seems a theoretical certainty that the articles system, reinforced by the rule that it should be uninterrupted for two years, is much more rational, if nothing else, than the often haphazard barrister's pupilage. It is also often useful to spend part of one's articles with a large London firm, even if one intends to practise in the provinces. With his principal's consent an articled clerk can spend up to one year during his articles with another solicitor.

Until about ten years ago it was still customary for a

principal to demand a premium from his articled clerk. This could be as much as £500 for a period of five years. But it is rare today for a premium to be payable. Indeed, a university law graduate should expect to be paid, up to a figure of £10 a week by the later stages of his articles. He, at any rate, after the initial few months of adaptation, should more than earn his keep. It need hardly be said that it does not follow from the fact that a premium is demanded that the firm is better than others.

Prospects of a Solicitor

It is as difficult to assess a practising solicitor's ultimate prospects as it is a barrister's. They vary in the same way with efficiency and ability. It has already been shown that he will have much greater security than a barrister. He will also start to earn money immediately. As an assistant solicitor with the firm to which he was articled, or elsewhere, he can expect to earn about £1300 a year in London, rather less in the provinces, and this should rise fairly rapidly. Most qualified men will be salaried solicitors for the first few years; some indeed will remain salaried for ever. A senior salaried man who has not entered into partnership can expect to earn about £3000 in London. But the average man will in due course either set up on his own account or purchase a practice or enter into partnership with others. In fact, he will usually become a partner. If so, he will, of course, have to purchase his share of the firm's capital and goodwill, and this will usually be done by deductions from his annual earnings.

The successful solicitor will not perhaps earn anything like the income made by the fashionable barrister. But it may be said perhaps that an average man in the middle range of the profession will earn about the same as his effective counterpart at the Bar, and he will also have the advantage of a higher degree of security and the ability to delegate, as well as something to sell when he retires. Also his practice may bring him into contact with business which may prove to be highly rewarding. All those things go to counterbalance the 'glittering prizes' of the Bar. At the same time, he will be obliged to maintain adequate offices and a competent clerical staff, and these things cost a great deal of money today.

Although judicial preferment is not available to a solicitor, there are some official appointments carrying salaries of up to £4000 or more a year open to solicitors of sound experience, such as Chancery Masters, Taxing Masters and Registrars of County Courts.

Government Service

A man is not bound to engage in private practice as a lawyer. There are other possibilities open to him. One in particular is a legal post in the government service. Most Government Departments have a legal staff and the posts are usually open to both barristers and solicitors. The starting salary is in the region of £1400 a year, and it goes up year by year; the senior posts may carry salaries of over £6000 a year. However, promotion is almost always on the basis of seniority. This may deter the very ambitious man, although there is, to offset this, a genuine security of tenure.

A man who has read law at the University has also the opportunity of entering the Administrative Class of the Home Civil Service. The examination, which is highly competitive and notoriously difficult, is open to all university graduates. The law graduate will therefore face the rivalry of products of other disciplines. There are about forty vacancies filled by competitive examinations every year. If he succeeds he will not work as a professional lawyer but purely as an administrative civil servant in an advisory capacity to Government Departments and Ministers. His progress should be more rapid than in the professional class, more store being laid on ability than seniority. With reasonable luck he should eventually expect to earn rather over £4000 a year and perhaps much more. Similar examinations are held for the Senior Branch of the Foreign Service.

Local Government

Every borough, county borough, urban district and rural district council has a Clerk. He is, almost invariably, the senior legal officer of the area. To a legally qualified man with an interest in social planning within a local setting the local government service offers highly attractive opportunities. There has been an occasional, but very rare, tendency in recent times to appoint a non-lawyer of proved executive ability to this post. Nevertheless, it is obvious that there will always be a considerable need for legally qualified men, and it seems reasonably certain that they will continue to command the great majority of important positions.

If a man is determined on a career in local government he will be well advised to serve under articles with a solicitor in the local government service, because the work is rather specialised. Barristers are rarely appointed. By no means all local authorities are willing to take articled clerks, but he should not, at any rate if he is a graduate, have too much difficulty in finding articles. Local authorities are often more generous in the way of remuneration to their articled clerks than solicitors in private practice. The starting salary for a qualified man may be slightly lower than in the professional civil service, but prospects are rather better, and promotion can be quite speedy. A Town Clerk of a large city may earn a salary of £6000 or more a year, and many qualified men earn salaries in the region of £3000 a year and above.

Industry and Commerce

This is an area of activity which varies enormously. Most of the large companies (as well as the nationalised industries) maintain a legal department. In private enterprise the starting salary may be rather higher than in the professional civil service or nationalised industry. On the other hand, there may be less security of tenure, though this depends very much on the company. Both barristers and solicitors are usually eligible for these positions. However, in the smaller company a solicitor has the edge over the barrister, because his training in common-form conveyancing or commercial work may be more appropriate to its needs. For example, he is perhaps more likely, all things being equal, to become a company secretary, if this is what he wants to be. On the other hand, in the very large concerns, such as the oil companies, a barrister with proven experience, particularly at the commercial or Chancery Bar, should be able to find a very suitable and well-paid niche.

But industry and commerce offer possibilities in fields other than professional law. An increasing number of law graduates enter business in the same way as other graduates are doing, as salesmen, managers, personnel officers and so forth; they may never practise in their profession, and may indeed never become professionally qualified.

Universities and Teaching

To those who are interested in teaching law and academic research it is the universities which have the greatest appeal. Most universities maintain a department of Law. But although the academic qualifications demanded are high, the salaries are rather lower than elsewhere. A man will start at £1200 as an Assistant Lecturer, and as Professor (the top rung of the ladder) he will earn about £4000 a year. However, these mundane facts are not of especial relevance to people with genuine academic inclinations.

The technical colleges and colleges of further education also often teach law. Oddly enough, although the academic qualifications required may well be lower, the starting salary is higher.

Women in the Law

In theory a woman has all the opportunities of a man in the legal profession. But it would be disguising reality to imagine that she has precisely the same chances. The true position is that, particularly in the practising branches of the profession, there is still a residue of prejudice against her. At the Bar she has to reckon with the reluctance of both professional and lay clients to instruct her, as well as the difficulty of entering effective chambers. However, things may now seem to be improving. A woman High Court Judge—Mrs. Justice Lane—has been appointed for the first time, and Miss Rose Heilbron, Q.C., has for several years acted as a Recorder of Quarter Sessions. Nevertheless, the fact remains that quite apart from the wastage caused by marriage, many women barristers drift away from the Bar, or alternatively remain on the fringe of the profession, spending most of their time, for instance, as law reporters or law publishers' readers.

The solicitors' branch is more favourable in this respect (partly because of the shortage of solicitors), and undoubtedly some women have become very successful solicitors. But there is still some difficulty in obtaining articles in the better firms. The position is best of all outside practice in salaried posts, and many qualified career women do tend to take a job of this kind.[1]

Suggested Reading

HENRY CECIL, *Brief to Counsel*, Michael Joseph.
H. J. B. COCKSHUTT, *The Service of a Solicitor*, Hodder & Stoughton.
RONALD RUBINSTEIN, *John Citizen and the Law*, Pelican.
GLANVILLE L. WILLIAMS, *Learning the Law*, Stevens.

NOTES

For further particulars about the profession generally, application may be made to the Under Treasurers of Lincoln's Inn, London, W.C.2, The Middle Temple, London, E.C.4, The Inner Temple, London, E.C.4 and Gray's Inn, London, W.C.1; the Council of Legal Education, Gray's Inn Place, London, W.C.1, and the Law Society, Chancery Lane, London, W.C.2.

Index